POETRY now

LIFE'S JOURNEY

Edited by

Steph Park-Pirie

First published in Great Britain in 2004 by
POETRY NOW
Remus House,
Coltsfoot Drive,
Peterborough, PE2 9JX
Telephone (01733) 898101
Fax (01733) 313524

SB ISBN 1 84460 829 8

FOREWORD

Although we are a nation of poets we are accused of not reading poetry, or buying poetry books. After many years of listening to the incessant gripes of poetry publishers, I can only assume that the books they publish, in general, are books that most people do not want to read.

Poetry should not be obscure, introverted, and as cryptic as a crossword puzzle: it is the poet's duty to reach out and embrace the world.

The world owes the poet nothing and we should not be expected to dig and delve into a rambling discourse searching for some inner meaning.

The reason we write poetry (and almost all of us do) is because we want to communicate: an ideal; an idea; or a specific feeling.

Poetry is as essential in communication, as a letter; a radio; a telephone, and the main criterion for selecting the poems in this anthology is very simple: they communicate.

CONTENTS

IF

If I could live my life again
I'd capture one moment of sweet sublime,
Then bottle it up and store it away
Until such time I could reminisce
With that moment of bliss.

If I could slow down the night
I would hold back the dawn.
When lonely ones waken to find lovers gone.
And all that is left is a memory.

If I could rekindle the flame in your eyes,
There would be no more heartaches, no more tears, no goodbyes.

This smallest of words, forever it seems,
Hauntingly drifts in and out of my dreams.
Forever reminding of what might have been.
If only.

Catherine Tidiman

PROZAC

The aftermath of summer's sweetness
Rose stemmed thorns amongst the flowers.
Strangling and erasing daydreams
Turning seconds into hours.
Winter's cold yet beckoning finger
Points to threads of icy chill
Which creep unseen on warm flesh resting
Solution, pop another pill.

On the surface I am smiling
Cheeks are chalky, eyes are dull.
Inside, I am slowly dying
Words erratic, hyper, low.
Autumn's solace fails to cheer me
Now I'm feeling tired and ill.
Stolen daylight, Duvet City
Solution, pop another pill.

I subscribe to this Prozac nation
Popping pills to dull the pain.
When even sunlight cannot filter
Through the depths of acid rain.
Even spring will not allure me
Rouse me from this numbing cold.
I'll retreat to warmer, welcome climates
First, I'll die and then grow old.

Deanna L Mills

REAPER

I know thou art there, for I sense thee.
I feel thy watchful eyes upon me.
Thou has time measured for each without equal length:
man, woman or child, thou has no favourites,
nor whims of compassion.
Thou dire consequence of foreboding affliction.
Mortality is man's greatest weakness,
and thou knows that man loves himself with too much kindness.

Thou does not pray upon his flesh,
for man has nothing left to sin.
For faith is the most fragile of virtues,
and thou dost know that man's flesh is weak and his soul too thin.

Yet thou dost wait, for thou art more God's servant than man.
Thou art beyond reproach, because thou know'st,
that love favours death when life becomes cruel;
for are not both created by God?
God can be cruel with his kindness.

Yet thou art the watcher, and thy gaze has been cast without time.
Only with man does it age.
For man is a creature that lives by time,
and thou art there to shorten his existence.

Nomad

SWEET AND SOUR

Sitting across from
the corner shop
I can see Burke inside
a big bug-eyed man
burly as a bear
white apron tied around
his barrel belly

large glass jars
on the counter top
filled with bulleyes,
chocolate centred satins
white coated bonbons
and Turkish delight

his fat hand groping
in the jar
he pops another bullseye
in his mouth
his tongue turning
a blue-black

my empty stomach
moans and whines
disturbed by the image
a sour taste in my mouth
I make my way home
up urine scented stairs.

Martina Quirke

TWO FOR ONE

From overseas I came in awe
To filch your loving country.
The first I noticed was a store
'Save and get a second free'.

When I have saved four ninety-nine
I'll grab a silly bargain
At two for one they will be mine
(Or should I learn the jargon).

Silly shoes seem such a giggle
At home they'll be delighted
English will get such a niggle
When I kneel and get knighted.

I've saved enough to start me off
So now I can get busy
They'll treat me like a super toff
I'll leave them all so dizzy.

First it's shoes, I've now saved enough
In the shop a size eight gem
Nice service too, they're not so rough
Two pairs for one, I've bought them.

Back to the bank I'll save and save
Until I've got the credit
I'm sure the saving will now pave
A path to show my merit.

So, two for one, I've banked again
To save and let it rip
To have enough to cause them pain
When I buy a battleship.

J Kay

A DEPRESSED DAY

This state.
God isn't present.
How does it begin? How did I get here?
I feel numb - oxymoron.
P***ed off
Pointless
Cruelty all around
Where did Love go?

I want to be alone.
Sod off world.
I do it to myself.
The world hasn't changed
It's me.
Pathetic.

There's no point to anything.
If Life's about experience,
Why can't I just experience nothing?
I *can!*

It all seems so fake.

What do I want to do now?
Who am I?

This stinks.
This state.

Ashley Tame

THE SONG OF THE WHALE

Big blue mountain in the sea,
Whale I heard you,
Grieving.
You can cry if you want
But you know we'll never let you be
And we'll never let you see,
Instead of life we choose
Lipstick for our painted faces,
Polish for our shoes.

Ammar Kalia (10)

ODE TO A YOUNGER MAN

A social night out with mutual friends our first meeting
You brought me a drink -
Whilst I was the life and soul of the evening
Entertaining the crowds!

Then you rescued me from an over amorous colleague
I found that rather endearing
And so I took you home with me
The way one befriends a stray puppy!

But once unleashed you were more like a tiger
Your lust and passion matching my own
Nice . . . and I thought that would be it
But rather cheekily you pressed your number
Into the palm of my hand

And so began a passionate affair
No strings - just great sex and lots of laughs
But we were similar in some ways
Shared star signs, similar humour matching sizzling passion
Hidden depths

Yet from my whole CD collection (300 in all)
You'd only ever heard of Fleetwood Mac and Lulu
And I realised I was old enough to be your mother
Guess that's the only downside to having a toy boy!

Sally Barker

THE DARK NIGHT

How dark is the night
And how deep is the ocean?
When the sun goes down at night
Then the moon stepped in
With her pleasant light
When all creatures, whether great or small
Are asleep, for it is night
The dark night
Then, awake in the morning
Bathe by the bright sun
Tell me
How dark is the night
And how deep is the ocean?

P B James

COUPLING

Two fish eager to spawn between sheet and duvet;
swimming on undercurrents of bliss,
we rise then fall then rise in a flood of passion,
clinging to each other we drift as we swell towards climax.

You place a cigarette between the fingers of your hand,
place it gently on your lips and puff,
searching for your second wind.
I watch the ruby-glow as you inhale.

Lying by your side I sip at sleep . . . you exhale . . .
I watch the blueness of smoke rings;
I place my lips on your skin, taste salty diamonds,
rekindle your embers . . .

Coupled once more we ride the white water of rapture.

J Spiers

SHIPMATES

People come and go,
I don't give a damn,
when I was about to go, another new batch came,
happy and smiling faces, for us, home at last,
naive and lonely faces, for those who just arrived.

While taking our lunch, I noticed you,
mopping the floor, you're not bothered at all,
so quiet, so sad, you don't seem to enjoy,
you're working harder in order to earn more.

The loner, the quiet man, that's what I thought of you,
what a pity, I didn't approach you, I should have done it earlier,
so I can understand you better. Some find you moody,
that is so noticeably, the others misunderstood you,
they always make you angry.

You're after all one brilliant mate, so close to God,
keeping the faith, we have a lot in common,
we tend to solve things on our own.
You are an ambitious and confident lad, like myself I'm really glad.

Can friends be soulmates? In that case, you are one great friend,
you touch my life and shared my every moment
of your secrets, fears and achievements.
Your fears are the same as mine,
your goal is so precious as time,
I like the way you perceive life
so easy, yet so deep
full of hopes, full of wishes.

Thank you mate for being there
for giving your time, effort and care
I will never forget the dreams we share
like two brilliant buddies, the perfect pair.

Lee N Fausto

LAND OF THE BIG SKY

Summer sun sinks
to bathe still waters,
in the land of the big sky.

Sultry breezes kiss the willow.

Fading light produces
dappled shade,
in the land of the big sky.

Lunar light explodes.

Nature's nightly chorus
rings out,
in the land of the big sky.

Slumber beckons.

David Lees

A DIP IN THE DEEP

What is the mind? Is it something in space,
a mystery forever undefinable?
Is it something universal, like life itself,
everywhere and nowhere, yet for everyone?
We know it's from the mind that our ideas come,
and that our brain directs the body to achieve them.
But what and where is the mind?

For a thing to exist it must have form!
So is the mind a sort of entity omnipresent and ubiquitous,
onto which once logged we are conscious,
and that life itself is just a state of being while connected?
Is the mind of every creature then, simply his brain logged on?
But what and where is the mind?

Is this really the truth, the reality,
a physical world in the main controlled by instinct,
a subtlety from nowhere directing each creature
to live out its span and fulfil the purpose of its life?
Really! Is there really some entity doling out perception
in variable amounts, playing mind games?
But what and where is the mind?

So what's it all for?
The atom, the particle, the molecules of matter,
the millions of mutations living out their lives through the years.
It's a mystery far beyond our understanding.
Then what of the end, the finality? Are our lives lived already?
Is our destiny fixed, our pathetic fumbles all for nothing?
Dust to dust, ashes to ashes, the spirit made flesh and all that.
But the question remains: What and where is the mind?

P Jennison

THE SPIDER'S WEB

It was such a dismal morning
All misty with fine rain
But hanging in my garden
Was something to bring a smile again
Between two tall plants
That stood like towers
Was a perfect spider's web
How busy was the spider
While I was in my bed
With no film in my camera
I could only stand and stare
At the lonely little spider
Patiently hanging there
His web is made so perfect
Like a crocheted table mat
And he sits in the middle
Not moving, but hoping that
Very soon a fly or insect
Will manage to be caught
Inside his lovely web
What a happy thought
I have never, ever seen
Such a perfect web before
So on this dismal morning
There's one thing that's for sure
I'm lucky to be able to look
And see outside my door.

D Fryer

PLEASE DON'T WAKE ME IF I'M DREAMING

Please don't wake me if I'm dreaming,
Please don't wake me, 'tis not true,
Tell me once again you love me
And you'll ne'er again be blue.

Hold me close to you, my darling,
Put your sweet lips soft on mine,
Treat me tenderly as always,
Tell me once again you're mine.

For if I am only dreaming, then all this cannot be true,
And you could not be loving me, the same as I love you,
And I would be so lonely if our love I could not keep,
So if I am only dreaming, then 'tis best you let me sleep.

Shirley Gray

I

Oh what, oh what's going on in my head?
I don't want to be living, I want to be dead
I've lived my life with a sense of achievement
Now I go on in a form of bereavement
I want a place where I'm happy and glad
And not to feel miserable and sad
All day long I sit and stare
Not giving a damn for the people who care
The people who love and want me well
Can't take me away from this living hell
How can I end this trouble and strife
The only way is to take my life
What will happen to those who love me
Maybe in time they will forgive me

My private thoughts of suicide
Are mine to keep and mine to hide
And if I'm asked if I'm OK
These thoughts I must keep locked away.

Maria Rousseau

LOST

Why do you cry, when you're on your own
When you're alone
In the darkness
Far away from home

Lost is you
With fear in your heart
You keep your secret hidden as you walk the cold path

No sympathy will you get
No kindness will you receive

Lost is you, without a name
A shadow
Of the path that is a mere memory

You are a memory
That should stay lost

There is no room for you
In my cold, dark heart

For, would you cry
If I stabbed you in the heart
When you are lost in the silence
Of the dark

You are worthy of misery
No friendly face will you see
Not even the kindest of stranger will help thee

For this is your fate,
Does it sound similar
For this is what you did to me
In the darkest
Of all hours.

Kayleigh Jones

NATURE

Nature's powerful majesty graces the eye
Silver birch and ancient oaks soaring high.
Flora evolves myriad, as if from Rafaelian brush
Winding streams meander as shadow falls hush.
A sunburst's shiny shaft bestrews a shy
Veiled cloud creating spiritual beauty by.
Visions yellow embrace their grassy host
Cowslips and meadow lush olivine boast.
Gaily, giddy and proud chestnut mare
Stands with her foal snorting morn's air.
Hedgerow 'pon hedgerow white pink bloom
Its blossom 'pon blossom mantled festooned.
The song of a throstle heard before dark
Set antiphon at morrow with linnet and lark.
In conception conflating with seasons four
Its rejoice will form creations awe.

Michael Maloney

ONE IN A MILLION

Thank you for being you
For everything you say and do.
For your love and friendship
Your smiles and charms
And the way, you hold me in your arms.
For the fun and laughter, joys and sorrows.
I love you, just as much today
As I will for all the tomorrows.
You are my darling
For all these reasons,
My one in a million.

David Skinner

DON'T KNOW HOW TO SAY GOODBYE

I suppose I will have to
Like you from a distance,
And hold onto my resistance.

I don't know why,
I don't know how
To say goodbye?

Even though so much time
Has gone it was
As though time
Has stood still.

Maybe even though I wanted to stay,
I thought I would
Save my love for
An even brighter day,
When someone new
Might come my way.

Because you just had
This hold over me,
That I could not explain
So all I could do was refrain.

I wish I had the strength
To say goodbye,
But I knew when I did
I was going to sigh.

Because you just had
This hold over me
That I could not explain,
So I had to leave it
To the cold pouring rain.

Diane Mangal

WEALTH

I am not rich
As this world reckons riches;
And yet within a hundred moss-lined ditches
I count the golden buttercups that shine,
And they are mine.

I have no store
Of what men deem as wealth;
And yet I have the priceless gift of health.
So while, by God's good grace, this treasure's mine,
Shall I repine?

I've no array
Of jewels, fine and rare;
But in the woods there's plenty - and to spare,
Of sapphire bluebells, diamond-tipped with dew,
For me - and you.

I do not own
A large and grand estate;
But family and friends around me wait,
And I've their love for my inheritance,
As recompense.

Muriel Rawson

The 'Experience' Mystery

I strolled downtown along Hospital Lane
And walked past the busy maternity wing
I thought I heard a weepy soprano voice sing
The pitch grew jerky and too throaty for a song
The cry of a mother who had in the past bore nine
I wonder why experience never calms one in pain

Early today we lost a life in the operating theatre
Our senior surgeon was doing his best to suture
He walked out distressed this morning at five
And confessed my brother had lost a dear wife
Despair severed through our hearts like a knife
I wonder when experience should save a mere life

Our team was trailing by just a few points
When someone fouled in the dying minutes
The coach looked through his long players' list
And picked an experienced dead-ball specialist
In a minute we all looked away in dire disgust
I wonder why goal experience is such a con artist

I was enrolled in this best class in the school
Where sharp minds were put to test like a tool
The master was one of the best known in time
So witty he was tried and tested like old wine
But the national examination result was so dismal
I wonder when experienced tutorship is so subnormal

A host of marriages break everyday, we hear
Most of them so cherished, legendary and so dear
Stretching back into time immemorial they stand
All the existing young couples fail to understand
Will their maiden relationships survive this dilemma?
I wonder why experience leads to such marriage drama.

Everson Mpofu

THERE'S A PLACE BEYOND THIS WORLD

There's a place beyond this world of ours,
Where the sky is always blue,
And the only kind of tears that flow are of laughter,
And there is so much love, too.
But you have to stay here
For many a year,
For some maybe only a few,
For there's things here we have to learn,
Our place in heaven to earn.
But whatever our age when we reach there,
Be it young or old,
So much happiness to behold,
That if you were told
To earth you could return,
You would say in a definite way,
'No, Lord, let me stay
Where there is rest and peace,
And happiness,
And laughter and love and no pain,
And the Lord always there to talk to, so near,
Here in eternity remain.'
So if I am no longer here,
Do not grieve for me and do not fear,
It is I for you who feel so sad,
For me you should feel only glad.
I know it hurts you that I am far away,
But trust in the Lord, we shall meet again one day.
So stay true to your faith, whatever the test,
Have faith in the Lord, and He will do the rest.
And when we meet again,
Then for yourselves you will see
Why there was no need to feel sad for me.

Pat Todd

I THINK THEREFORE

Floating in suspension, in a state of apprehension,
Gazing at swirls gathering in to be part of some question
Have I become, I wonder why
And contemplate as I float by.

Concern arises as in an infinite void,
I continue to float without substance in all things,
An invisible thing on invisible wings.

Putting these thoughts to the back of my conscious,
Drifting along devoid of essence,
In a state of transparency, lost to infinity,
Bursting asunder, in a transient state of wonder.

Expanding now at a rapid rate,
No sense of being, no time, no date,
Can this be? Is it a sham?
Impossible. I think, therefore I am.

Surrounded by lights, many hot, many bright,
All flying away at incredible speed,
As though on a journey of some great need.

With an urgency to differentiate,
With increased consternation I deliberate and equate,
How can I expand at this impossible rate?

In panic I become confused, has my mind been abused?
Suddenly things fall into place, this is a trivial race,
This is my being, this is my aim, I am the whole, I am the van,
The very beginning is what I am, steady state, big bang.

To know what I am is of great import to me,
To know what I am, to know that I be.
Apprehension has gone, I am not the adverse
I am the beginning, I am legion,
I am the universe.

K Dennett

THE TEARS OF TURIN

Should I fail to love thee all flowers would die,
And the Araby shores would be seen in the sky -
With a thousand white horses astride of the waves,
And all the world's kings would be turned into slaves;
The rivers return to the source of the rain,
And the 'Tears of Turin' would be flowing again -
Should my love for thee wane.

So never say never, nae never my friend,
My love holds forever, true to the end.

And should thou too love me all flowers would grow,
And tears of joy to the rivers would flow;
The rivers would snake their way to the sea,
Where the Araby shores would be waiting for me,
And astride a white horse I would reach down for thee,
And twixt surf and the stars forever we'd be -
Should thou too love me.

So say forever, aye ever my friend,
Wilt thou love me forever, true to the end.
And should there be such a thing as 'The Tears of Turin',
Shed for the right reason t'would not be a sin.

Roger Oldfield

ITCHING TO TELL

Charlie Flea married Betty Flea
and they lived on an old black cat,
where the fur was smooth and homely,
so they call it their pussy flat.
Now I'm glad to tell they lived quite well,
and got on with their neighbours, George and Nell.
They had quite a family as time went by
and moved to a penthouse, way up high
between the ears of the old black cat
where Betty Flea grew big and fat.
Now Charlie Flea got itchy feet
and hopped away into the street
where he jumped aboard a nanny goat
who was going to sea in an open boat,
which finally landed on a foreign shore,
poor Charlie had never been abroad before,
so he jumped on a monkey which he thought was a cat
and was eaten for breakfast, and that was that.

John Tovey

SKIN DEEP

She's classy, she's brassy
She thinks she's really bright
She cons the men to jump the queue
Same time, same place, same night
Her make-up is immaculate
You'd think she's headline news
But God forbid if you should drop
Your ale on her Jimmy Choos
The women watch in jealousy
She just ignores their spiteful glares
Her beautiful sculptured body
Attracts admiring stares
Drinks lined up like railway carriages
Once gone another reappears
Have not the heart to tell him then
You are not as young as your years!

Jacqueline Taylor

THE GHOSTLY HOUSE

Thunderstorms and wind howls
Deep in the bowels.
Lightning flashes and the sea bashes
Against the rocks.
The doors creak and windows slam.
Stairs creak and rats squeak.
Wolves howl and spiders crawl.
Ghosts moan in the hall.

Steven Fearnley (12)

FATHER

You make me so proud
In everything you do
I hope that when I'm older
I end up just like you.

You taught me right from wrong
You taught me good from bad
For the past twenty years
You have been a great dad.

I hope that the future
Brings just as much joy
I'm becoming a man
No longer a boy.

So when I need help
I know you'll be there
To offer your support
And to show love and care.

Gary Bil

WINNING

To run until your lungs are fit to burst
To strive so hard simply to be first.
To climb the mountain to the summit
And to feel that there's no limit.
To all the things that you can do
To feel that you can never rest
Must put your strength to every test
And always, always come out best.
But sometimes best is not enough
Try to be of sterner stuff
Choose instead to put self last
And let another win
For could it really be a sin?

I Wilson

A RAILWAY JOURNEY

Sitting on the train all on my own,
Not making a sound, not wanting to moan.
All the children from London are being sent away,
To go off to the country to stay.
Now the smoke starts to bellow and off we go,
And the carriage starts humming to and fro.
I look out of the window and see meadows whizz past,
Full of cattle and sheep, the numbers are vast.
As we rush past the town the church bells ring,
The town looks so peaceful, such a wonderful thing.
As we start to slow down and the station comes into view,
The other children get excited like monkeys in a zoo,
I smile to myself and think of my journey,
Then rush onto the platform to meet my new guardians Jill and Berny.

Heather Tarplee (11)

OUR GREEN

Cannot believe what I have seen today.
They have taken our beautiful green away.
Where children play on the swings and the slides.
Going on the roundabout, enjoying the rides.

Nice place to take the dogs for a walk.
Stop, have a chat, meet for a talk.
Now someone has bought it, we don't know who.
Must be a developer, that's what they do.
Wants to build houses, factories as well.
Maybe some flats, too soon to tell.

Here comes the diggers to churn up the ground.
Out go the swings and the merry go round.
Gone are the trees, that once gave us shade.
The leafy path, that led to the glade.

Even the wildlife, robbed of their home.
All they can do, is wander and roam.
Why do people have to be so greedy.
They obviously have no thought for the needy.

Now there is nowhere to go for a walk.
Meeting the neighbours, stopping to talk.
Taking away our beautiful green
Just to replace it with something obscene.

Joan Morris

GETTING OLD

I feel so weary, I must go to bed,
But a hundred thoughts churn through my head.
Have I switched everything off? I ask myself,
Now what are my shoes doing on the shelf?
My head feels woolly, my legs feel lame,
I wonder if that friend of mine feels the same.
Oh no, not her, she is only seventy-nine,
I would like to see her at the age of mine.
What am I saying? She is older than me,
No wonder I feel so bad, I can hardly see.
Maybe what I need is a nice cold drink,
But what is this? My specs I think.
Hooray, hooray, I am not blind,
Now what was that I tried to find?
Oh go to bed, why worry so?
But I need my shoes, don't you know?
I toss and turn and cannot sleep,
I must have counted every one of those sheep.
I close my eyes, 'Dear Lord,' I pray,
'Please help me and guide me in every way.
I am still your child even though I'm old,
I want you to take me and in your arms enfold.'

Marie Knott

TWO ARTFUL DODGERS

An Artful Dodger was Toby,
He pinched what he could find,
Small hankies of tissue or cotton,
He never minded which kind.

An Artful Dodger is Sally,
She steals a night dress case.
Pyjamas and jackets and bedsocks -
She loves to be in disgrace.

An Artful Dodger was Toby;
He's stolen many balls
From people when playing at cricket,
He liked to hear frantic calls.

An Artful Dodger is Sally;
A slipper locked in jaws,
She'll chew it as if it's for supper,
Then hold it fast in her paws.

Two Artful Dodging cockers,
Their snouts in people's bags
Just searching for something of interest
Two most experienced lags!

An Artful Dodger was Toby,
To him it was a game.
Now Sally follows his footsteps -
An Artful Dodger the same.

Dorothy J Stirland

HOUSEBOUND

Trains rattle by as I sit at my window
I wonder who is on, and where they do go.
Maybe it is for pleasure or maybe just work
Will they get hurt if it stops with a jerk?
It is a long time since I was on a train
Nowadays it is too much of a strain
You see I am unable to move
Yet I fancy myself flying like a dove
Listening to noises and seeing movement
Is a great joy, if just for a moment
When you are housebound and on your own
Life can get lonely, always living alone
But do not think I am sad, or envy the fit
They cannot just leave things like me and have a good sit
We are not all miseries because we are unfit
We would just like help, now and then a little bit
So next time you see an old dear at a window
Give her a wave and a smile as you go
Then she will know that at least she has been seen
And feel still alive and not just a has-been.

Anne Roach

MY FICKLE MAID

Sweet it was to glance into bright eyes
That answering, reflected into mine;
An ecstatic change of kindred sighs,
With each a name to call to mind.

Sweet it was then to go a-walking
With smiles like summer sunshine shed;
Then to wander home, remembering
Secret things that each of us had said.

But all that sweetness was nothing worth,
When salt tears bedimmed its fading life;
Though 'twas gracious even at its birth,
Love set so soon - became a darkest night.

Am I pessimistic? If you will,
To have loved in such a sugared mood,
And suffer then the bittering pill
Of a maiden's false and lying word.

The truth then I learned - be slow to trust!
Fickle maidens' minds do swiftly change;
In dalliance changing hearts to dust -
Hands to empty gloves and eyes estranged.

Philip J Tonkin

THE FOLLY OF MAN

God created the earth, sea and sky
He endowed it with forests and mountains, towering on high
Creatures wild and roaming free
And birds sang joyful melodies

For many years there was peace in the land
Then greed and enmity took a hand
In the form of man, who was also given life
For many a long year, there was nothing but strife

Nation fought nation throughout the ages
But, still they don't learn from history's pages
Man creates his own hell here on Earth
When it could have been so different, the land of their birth

When will it cease, all of this slaying?
Man killing man, with no thought of paying
The ultimate price, as finally, they wend
To face their maker at journey's end.

E Gallagher

YOU ARE MY LOVE

You are my love, my only love and I wish that you were here
I want to kiss and hold you, if only you were near
I think about you every night when I'm tucked up in bed
About the good times we had and all the things we said
I know that you must miss me and I miss you as well
And when you come home for good we will take the wedding vow
And so my darling this note's to say, keep thinking of me every day
And very soon the time will come when we will be together
And our hearts will be as one.

Dee Wheeler

SUMMERTIME

It is raining again, it is raining,
It is summer, in old London Town,
At least you can tell, that it's summer,
The rain it is warm, coming down.

When you get up, on a June morning,
The weather it is raining, and cold,
In the afternoon, it is snowing,
You dress up, to go to the Pole.

The sun, then makes an appearance,
Making everyone, happy and gay,
Sunbathing, with winter coats on,
Four seasons, all in one day.

W J R Dunn

My Love

Often in the night I've cried
When I think how strong you were by my side,
Playing and laughing being as one
Running in the meadow having lots of fun.
I was your princess, you were my king
So much in love it made our hearts sing
But now the pain is hard for you
I see it in your face and it makes me blue.
Once you walked proudly, now you stumble
But never once do you ever grumble.
I push your wheelchair every day
Looking down at hair that now is grey.
People stare as we go down the road,
I want to shout, 'He's not a heavy load.
We're together and we don't care.'
Whatever happens in life we'll share
Because I'm your queen and you're my king.
The love we have is everything.
As long as we're together, I'll always be glad
Because my life without you would make me sad.

Bridget Skeels

MY DAD

(This poem is dedicated to my dad, John Harold Beardmore)

Why oh God did he have to die.
If I said I don't miss him it would be a lie.
One minute he was there the next he was gone.
In my opinion he was second to none.

His cheery smile said everything was okay.
Everything, that is until today.
You knew he was there, when you needed a friend.
He was there when I needed him right to the end.

He taught me how to love and care.
When I was unhappy, he was always there.
When I helped around the house he was glad.
When I failed my exams he was sad.

Now he's gone it's hard to cope.
We'll meet again some day I hope.
The next time you think your dad doesn't care
You'll realise he did, when he's no longer there.

Lynda Carol Beardmore

DREAM

Dream about wonderful things
Dream about what life brings,
Dream a perfume of the finest flower,
Dream of a knight in an ivory tower,
Dream of the love between you and me,
Dream of the happy times we have seen,
Dream of the memories we have together,
Dream of the years we spend forever,
Dream of the finest web of love,
Sent to us from Heaven above,
Dream your dream and may it be pleasant,
For it is like the vast desert,
Your dreams will go on forever and ever,
Your love for each other will not sever.

Susan Ferrett

A SUNNY WAY

It was a very sunny way
to start a most unusual day,
the walls away, did melt in air,
on waking in a forest there,
I sat up rather quickly, and
a tray of food was in my hand,
sweet breakfast lashings all about
and flowers swaying, in and out,
thick clouds rolling overhead,
a sea of daisies round my bed,
an angel standing at my feet,
a smile upon her face to greet
me, on my rising, she did say,
'This is in fact a pleasant way
to start your morning, and too, mine,
may I join you as you dine?'
'Of course,' I smiled, with syrup dripping
down my chin, from too much sipping,
'But why all this, how can it be?'
Her reply, 'I had this morning free,
and angels roll in pleasure giving,
flipping eggs and flour sieving,
breakfast makes me smile and too,
the sky this morn was far too blue
to go on sleeping, or eat inside,
I thought you'd like this countryside.'
'Indeed, it pleases all I am
to wake within this angel land,
in fact I like it oh so much,
may we again come here, for lunch?'

Debbie Smith

ATTITUDES

Tolerance breeds a comfort zone
When all around, there's fighting talk
Actions modestly displayed
Create a patience, never overwrought.

Looking at gratitude, we owe our friends
Loving feelings, life and its trends
Gracious livings, spacious misgivings,
Happiness lies where only truth survives.

Overindulgence - blowing the gaff
Neither relates to harmony, but strife
Attention to details, giving your best,
Driving a bargain, or taking a test.

Strong in the mind - resisting arrest,
Leaving someone stranded, don't care a damn.
Feelings of hatred, bitterness - and sham
Causes of hopelessness, defeat, or staying just as I am.

Albert Boddison

TEACHERS

Teachers teach you everything you need to know,
They teach you English, maths, and even how to sew.
They teach you art, how to sketch and paint,
They teach you RE from a priest to a saint.

Teachers teach children, at least thirty,
When it snows they come in dirty.
Teachers come from all over England,
They can even come from a country called Finland.

Amy Clancy (9)

ARCHIE'S PET
(You scratch my back: I'll scratch yours)

Little Archie Gray
Had a pure white mouse,
He decided to take it to school one day
To give it a change from the house.

Archie placed his little mousy
Inside his desk with some breadcrumbs,
Teacher entered the room so Archie, grousy,
Settled down to do his sums.

Soon Archie heard his pet scratching
But too high did he lift the desk lid,
And just when he thought no one was watching
His mouse scrambled out from where it hid.

Crumbs of cheese
It preferred to nibble,
And such it would seize
Without a quibble.

It just so happened that the teacher's snack
Consisted of cheese rolls upon that day;
On the table they stood in a paper pack -
A feast for a beast, you might say.

So when the mouse smelt double Gloucester
It didn't hang around to beg,
And as the teacher marked the roster
The mouse scurried up her stockinged leg.

Shocked and shaken to the core
And letting out a horrendous shriek
Teacher ran for her life through the classroom door
Screaming, 'Class dismissed! Eeek!'

Archie, mouse, and all their friends too -
As the outcome of this prank -
Went to the seaside and strolled through the zoo,
To his pet Archie said, 'I've got you to thank.

A trip to the seaside, a trip to the zoo,
You did me and my friends a favour;
So on the way home I'll buy just for you
A pound of cheese in your favourite flavour.'

Teresa Kelly

DON'T WRITE ANYMORE

Today I woke up and the day was bright and fresh,
But I was laden with conundrums of deep dreams.
Birds sang on amongst green trees entwined like mesh,
And the bees swarmed flowers in reams.

In my dream I saw endless roads in a maze of tar,
But the absence of cats' eyes did not reassure.
The pavement loomed up and met with my car,
But still I dreamed on of your radiant allure.

A dream you remain although it must be said
The loss of your beautiful morning smile,
And the cold hollow of your shape in my bed,
Reminds me my only comfort is to wait awhile.

It was a preference for us to go out on a limb
Consequence not crossing our minds,
If only I'd known it was like putting my heart in a sling
Regardless of all the good signs.

All the adoration I possess can't satisfy you,
And for this I truly am sorry.
I really thought I could be your 'one in a few'
And not only your argument and quarry.

Good times will come and they will go,
And this I must always accept,
In spite of my perseverance although
There' snot even hope of friendship left.

Stellio Coutsides

THE RAINBOW APPEARED

On a hillside one bright sunny day,
A rainbow appeared to the children of God.
'Pray for peace to save the world,'
The words did say, spoken and heard.
Heaven's doors are in the sky,
So find the ladders so high.

G P Louch

TIME

There's a time to laugh, a time to cry,
a time to say a fond goodbye,
a time to love but not to hate,
a time to make up before it's too late.

There's a time to say, 'I love you',
before she turns way,
there're many things you can't put off
until another day.

Time is short, so much to do,
so use it very wisely,
don't be a fool, don't throw it away,
above all things, find time to pray.

Keith Slatter

TIMES LIKE THESE

The radio's playing
Soft music in the air
The room is warm
The lights are low
All of us are there
We chat and laugh
And talk about
The things we've done today
Everybody listening
To what the other has to say
The atmosphere is calm
Relaxed
Just how it should always be
It's times like these
You want to make
The moment last forever
For what you've got
Is worth much more
Than any gold or treasure.

Tracy Telfer

ANNABEL'S BIRTHDAY

We know a lass called Annabel
who's five years old today,
but still she's had to go to school -
can't stay at home to play.
We bet she's had some lovely gifts
and no doubt she's had some sweets,
but she mustn't eat them all at once
or her dinner she might not eat.
We say, 'Happy birthday, Annabel'
and send lots of love to you,
we hope that we will see you soon.
Mum, Dad and Izzie too.

Sue Hill

No Regrets

I'm sat here, quite lonely,
Decrepit and old,
In absolute silence
And feeling the cold.

A glance in the mirror,
What do I see there?
Wrinkled, leathery skin
And snowy-white hair.

Yet, once I was robust,
A tall, handsome brute,
And all the young ladies
Thought I was so cute.

So, how has it happened
That I've gone downhill?
It isn't grand living,
Bad luck, lack of skill.

The root of the problem,
To cause such decay,
Is just life's rich pattern
That got in the way.

Instead of complaining,
I'm glad to relate,
I'm healthy, contented,
And life is still great.

Brian M Wood

A WALK WITH THE MOMENTS

Moments fly, the eyes cry . . .
The laughter is a façade . . .
I don't even know why?
I sit by the window . . .
I wait for my dream . . .
The night engulfed it . . .
Can't even hear the scream . . .
A roll of dice, a sad demise . . .
The smile that was real . . .
Somehow turned to ice . . .
The truth, the lies . . .
Play a game . . .
But I'm not wise . . .
They take me to a land . . .
Where I believe I'm free . . .
But the tangled web, the mirage . . .
I just can't see . . .
And so, I'm walking with the moments . . .
And this is my journey
- *the peregrine.*

Snehal K Chokhandre

OCEAN

Rain-spattered salty air
Harshly flecks face and eyes
Churning, grey vast solitaire
Boiling cauldron on the rise

Squall and spume disputing
Ancient rocks uprooting
Tears and teardrops distending
Tides and time never-ending

Created in his glory
Land and sea, side by side
Eternally receding
Then returning
Crashing the incoming tide

Paul Reed

MY CHILD

As you grow,
My child,
May I have the strength to give you
The courage
To face life's obstacles,
The wisdom
To make the right decisions,
The confidence
To be at peace with who you are,
The peace
To love unconditionally,
The understanding
Never to discriminate,
The appreciation
Of life and all things beautiful,
The commitment
To be the best person you can be,
The patience
Never to be complacent about anything,
The skills
To listen, understand, love, sympathise
And never to judge anyone.
And as you grow,
My child,
I will fill your life with my love,
And I will give to you
All that I am
And all that I can be . . .

Julie Marvin

CHANGES OF THE SEASONS

Untouched virginal and white -
Winter that requested interlude -
A break with time and fantasy,
A mirror on the landscape,
Snow on the ground
From changed seasons.
The fall of the leaves in autumn -
So many coloured changed on Earth's bed
A key of the season in operation -
Sculptured images
Looking back on nature
In its own colour print.
Tranquillity in silence
To the passive swan down stream or river.
Nature in all beauty and sound -
Love's own harvest.

Roger Thornton

GYPSIES SING

Gypsies sing and dance by the fire
They trade clothes and jewellery for money
They even predict your future. There's something
exciting about gypsies but yet
frightening too.

We are told never to turn a gypsy away
because they may curse you

But this is just a myth, so don't worry too much
about it.

Gypsies are wild, pretty and interesting and
each have a tale to tell round the campfire, it
seems to me a gypsy's life is a hard life.

Debbie Storey

MEMORY

A lovely lady I knew for years,
We shared laughter and a few tears
Right from my childhood and beyond
She forged a link, a chain, a bond
And showed me what was right from wrong
She was so gentle yet so strong
She worked hard all her life,
She had known both good and strife
Her hours long, her wages poor,
Yet she turned no one from her door.
She was the same to friend or foe,
A need for help, to her they'd go,
She had her faults, but should you call
She'd do her best for one and all,
I thank you Lord, you gave to me
A richness more than I could see
So undeserving was I then,
You called her back to you again.
But all those years up to the end
She was my mother and my best friend.

E M Housman

PEEPING THROUGH

I can peep through the Venetian blind
With eyes like matchsticks.
I can see you, you are blurred.
Yes, I know I tend to soar you to the heavens -
But always when you're not there to remind me.

If you come to the open window, face to face,
I plummet to the floorboards.

My darling you can never be he.
How unfair to shoot the pedestal so high.
How can you be the Empire State building
When you're nearer St Paul's . . .
Or even at times, the biscuit factory?

Today is the first day.
Today I am on a shiny stage.
I know about the rippling water,
It hurtled under the bent bridge
Along with Rick's Café American.

My old slippers are full of new toes.
Somebody's eyes need not worry,
I saw a rejuvenation
And found a centrifuge of lost ideals.
I leapt to catch the ride
And became dizzy.

I don't need.
I'll cut the tug-boat rope
And kick the vessel ashore.
Never return to steal affection.

Let sleeping dogs lie
While peeping dogs leap,
Lusting for the ocean
Tasting the salt spray.

Catherine Pasek

FIRST MEETING

One day has passed since I saw you last
And already I feel like an eternity has passed
I count down the days to see you again
To let go of the tears and be rid of the pain

To have you hold me again the way you did
Warmed my whole being, brought out that lost kid
I understand now that you have always loved me
But you were wrong when you thought I had a happy life by the sea

The past is gone and the future is here
And I feel good, I've confronted my fear
I now know that I was never rejected by you
And the events that happened in the past, it's all genuine and true

I feel sad though for all those lost years
But it's the future that matters now
Let's keep talking and be honest and true
Find out about each other, you about me and me about you

You will never know how complete you have made me feel
My past and future are finally real
It's all because of you Dad, so I say thanks
For never giving up hope.

I will never again be a stubborn goat . . .

Sue Burrows

FOUR KINGS

Three kings met to discuss the question of power
And one of them said, 'In fear of me, my subjects
Shake with such speed before my eyes
That I am barely able to see them.'
Another said, 'I live in tents - my palaces shook so much
In fear of me, that they are shattered.'
And the third said, 'My kingdom constantly quake in fear of me.'
With these words, something impenetrably dark
Rose from the court floor, and for a moment,
The kings felt weightless.
In terror, they shook so violently that,
Together with the dark ghost, dissolved in thin air
That stood like a lake on columns of light.

Alex Chobur

DEATH

Lacking in energy, his bones are brittle.
Robbed of speech, he utters little.
He's lying on a bed of thorns,
Shrivelled skin, life of scorn.
The colourful days never seem to last,
Are now distant memories flown past.
Mingled with confusion, crumbled of strife,
Boldly he still craves for life.
Flinching, he cannot bear to contemplate,
Death casts a shadow over his fate.

Shazia Kausar

THE LAST LAUGH

What was it that made you target me?
Competence, popularity - I still fail to see
Why you wore me away, like water on a stone.
Whatever I did you ensured that I was alone,
Alienated, like a wounded animal left to die.
Was it because I refused to cry?

Workplace bullies have no shame,
To them torment is just a game.
Mental anguish gave way to pain
What on Earth did you think you would gain?
It seemed as if the loaded gun held to my head
Was my way out - I should be dead.

Well now the last laugh is on you
Barristers and the like, took a very dim view
To your dastardly deeds.
You are the ones who now pay for my needs.
The pressure is off, I do what I can
No targets to meet, nor answer to any man.

I finally live my life in my garden and home
Visit the seaside, splash in the foam.
Play with my cat,
Watch him sleep on his mat.
Oh yes, early retirement has been good to me
At last - I am content with all that I see.

Theresa M Carrier

THE OPPOSITE SEX

If I had a potion to read a man's mind
I think I would be fascinated by what I would find
Is it true what the experts say
And men think about sex all day?

It's far more likely they think about sport,
Or playground battles as children they fought
Perhaps being an explorer is top of the list
Maybe of adolescence, and their first tantalising kiss.

Whatever men think about is secret to them
Like a hidden treasure chest in a pirate's den
Alas, there's no magic potion to jump in my man's head
But I suppose I find out most of his secrets when he leads me to bed.

C J Fulton

OH BUTTERFLY!

The sky greys in mimic of the pain down,
Of my garden, idyllic in its uniform brown.
But oh, what's this? A fallen cloud sculpted for show?
Its colours parting tears of a loath rainbow?

Whatever it be, a gush of beauty nigh!
It flies, it's alive, ah it's a butterfly!
As the azure dims the sun in vain,
Tall greens stoop to grasp the colourful stain!

Carried by the gasps of the wind,
Yes, tell me how he has sinned!
Gracefully evading the miasma of lust,
Tired wings rest, tempting the morals of dust!

Blind be the winter to your charms,
As the foliage hoards away the warm,
From pupa to caterpillar, pangs of unfold,
Many hues now, but don't you miss gold?

As you thieve the sun in sordid blazonry,
The jejune trail piqued in your wanton hurry!
The bloom seduced, the dew a forsaken mate,
Its fall cushioned by the earth's green pate!

A colourful cabaret in every coquette and flirt!
Every flower's paramour, nature's chastity in dirt!

I've no façade of a petunia or a daffodil,
No fragrance to entice you, but still,
Can't you hear my forlorn sigh?
O wings, do blunder! O butterfly, do flutter by!

Rajiv Sankaranarayanan

WEDDING DAY

I give to you all my heart,
This is the day our new lives start,
Upon my finger you place a ring,
I hear a choir of angels sing,
You have made my dreams come true,
I will always give my love to you,
This is the day I've waited for all my life,
For today we became husband and wife.

Sandy Ward

UNTITLED

I miss you.
      Staring into your brown eyes filled me with hope.
      My bringer of joy.
Happiness.

I miss you.
      Your black ruffled hair, which comforted me always.
      My blanket of warmth.
Protection.

I miss you.
      Your cheerful smile no matter what.
      My best friend always.
Love.

I miss you.
      But you're always in my heart.
      My poppy.
      We are together forever.

Katie-Leanne Findlay

CHARMING THINGS

There's a white horse, quick spit on your shoe,
Don't pass on the stairs, whatever you do.
A new moon through a window never glance,
Nor walk under ladders, why take the chance?
To safeguard against any black Fridays,
Remember to carry a rabbit's foot with you always.
Find a four-leaf clover, maybe a horseshoe,
To ensure that Lady Luck then shines on you.
Wishbones, black cats, even a lucky charm,
Are by tradition protecting us from harm.
I hear you ask, 'Why all this fuss?'
Why? It's because I'm superstitious!

Sue Hetherington

THE HEALING

In one moment of time
It all happened
The world that was known
Just disappears
Light becomes
We become full of tears
Yet, we do not perish
There are, new things to inherit
A form of bravery takes place
No waste, less taste
Or just find tranquillity
Life find a new ability
Others' sufferings just the same.

Never give in to silence
Listen as hard as you can
Then all becomes so clear
We can all feel less guilty
There are no doubts, no tears
We all feel less queer
Just that humble feeling
Heavenly things are still there.

Winifred Parkinson

TUG OF WAR FOR SANITY

As I sidestep to the left,
Sidestep to the right
I shift from the masks of my existence
I prove that I am not blessed
With anti-blending-in resistance.
Trying so hard to not conform
That I blank my state of mind.
Finding that any piece of peace of mind
Is so hard to find,
If you are forever in a battle.
Your nerves shaken like a rattle.
Confusion. Dilemma. Panic,
Too many question marks saddle
My attempts to milk my thoughts like cattle.

What make the man?
Clothes, character, or the skin?
Who lied to you and told you
Character is only skin-deep?
Who care the who we condemn
If in the end we all commit the same sin?
But maybe it is more forgivable
When it is one of us -
Than when it is one of them
Who came by foot, air or bus?

Sinners, forgivers,
Believers, non-believers
Leaders, please forgive us
To which god must I pray?
Upon which god will I my troubles lay?
My god or your god?
Your god or no god?
No god or sun god?
My belief system being dismantled

The contents of my consciousness
That I have to face every day
Questions and their issues
In my mind play and replay

My conscious interrogating me
So what have I done for the struggle?
Has just buying a Ché Guevara shirt
Done anything for a revolution revival?
Has writing a poem on my issues
Done anything for our survival?
Then I begin to question my conscious
So what have you done for the struggle?
Who is the struggle against?
Who is this enemy I haven't faced?
Is it racism or sexism?
Capitalism or Mugabe's Zim?
Is it the devil or your god?
Your god or no god?
No god or sun god?
Is the enemy you?
Maybe the enemy is me?
How do you expect me to believe in your God?
When I can't even believe in myself?
Isn't all your hatred going to eat me inside?
If my own conscious is fighting me
To whom will I confide?

The contents of my consciousness
That I have to face every day
Questions and their issues
In my mind play and replay

Play and
Replay and

Rewind

The contents of my consciousness
That I have to face every day
Questions and their issues
In my mind play and replay

Play and
Replay and
Never stop.

Mabel Mnensa

YOU ARE THE BEST AND I LOVE YOU

I've got your back, you've got mine,
I'll help you out anytime.
If I see you hurt, or I see you cry,
It makes me weep
And want to die.
And if you agree to never fight,
It wouldn't matter who's wrong or right,
If a broken heart, needs a mend,
I'll be there to the end.
If your cheeks are wet
From drops of your tears,
Don't you worry,
I'll keep you safe from all of your fears.
Hand in hand, love is sent,
We'll be together
Till the end.

Kirsty Bergin

FOREVER

I can't spend another lonely day without you,
the days are getting longer, the nights becoming blue.
I weep silently, but the tears fall gently on my pillow,
as they spread out, like the vines on a weeping willow.

All my life I have waited for the one true love,
and like an angel, God sent you to me from above.
You engulfed my soul, filled it with love and desire,
my heart beating anew, as it dances within your fire.

You breathe into me your love, and the sensations begin to arrive,
as I awaken to the senses, and start to feel so alive.
You have given me a reason to believe in something new,
all your sweet loving words, you whisper to me true.

The rhythm of your heart, beats in tune with mine,
as we descend into the depths of love, a feeling so divine.
As your soul melts into me, at last we become one,
two halves of the same spirit, we can't be undone.

We were written in the stars baby, destined to be forever,
and then fate played its part, when it brought us together.
I love you so much, and you're the reason that I live,
to fill your life with happiness, is my promise to you I give.

Nicola Spencer

LONELINESS

Here alone
Though not yet consumed by loneliness
I dream away another day
Gently cocooned into the
Bosom of my thoughts
Wistfully embraced by feelings
And caressed into the realms of my memories
The journey back never fails
To bring comfort or offer hope.

The past as it stands in its gloried apparel
Offers in its safe arms a deliverance
Which the present and future always fail to provide
Preferring instead to keep it
Hidden enigmatically away.

The present stands in the middle
And casts a murky shadow over my locked embrace
With a hand gripped to my shoulder
And a voice within my ear
'Leave the past to rest dear, don't you know it's for the best?'
My entwined fingers are prized away
And I regretfully return to
The presence of uncertainty.

Meanwhile the future
Slopes slyly around the corner
Like a recoiled spring ready to pounce.
Safe in the knowledge his time will come
An arrogant smile
Temptations to beguile
And pitfalls to lead the way.

Danielle Mulvaney

MY GRAVEST DAY

Was '83, the month of May,
turned out to be my gravest day.

Up at three to do my term,
watching the main engines turn.

The boat a routine surface made,
incoming signals to be relayed.

My name was called by intercom,
'To manoeuvring please do come.'

Ascending from the bowels below.
'Signal for me? Oh no! What a blow!'

It must be bad, there be no doubt,
that's what signals are all about.

A transfer made of the north-west,
to get me home they'll do their best.

From launch to car, and then by train,
my homeward journey was such a drain.

At Lime Street station I met my kin
who welcomed me and filled me in.

My journey's end, at last I'm home,
I see my mum, just skin and bone.

'Hello Mum,' I solemnly cried.
'Hello Al,' she whispered and died.

A Richardson

WHY?

Why do people hurt others so much
a nasty word, a look, or a touch?
Why can't people love and be friends
no more hatred, make amends?
Why not care about your fellow man?
It's not hard, if you want, you can.
Why not be nice and thoughtful, caring and kind?
Anyone can do it if they have half a mind.
Why not stop all the wars and love one another?
We are all human beings despite our colour.
Why does religion cause so much woe?
Let's try live in harmony and show
why we can be humble and forget and forgive
and let the whole world be friends
for as long as we live.

Lesley Hibbert

BRITISH SOCIETY

Shining roads and misty spires
The smell of rubber from the screeching of tyres
Lollipop ladies ready to pounce
Black and white humbugs sold by the ounce

It's eight o'clock and the kids are awake
Central heating for breakfast, mustn't be late
Parents with quilts on, scraping their cars
The council is gritting, giving grip to their tyres

Sitting on motorways, waiting in jams
The daily routine for the suburban man
Listening to the radio, the news and the chat
Pinpointing hold-ups, the weather and that

Accountants and business people playing sardines
Pinstripes and brollies, immaculately preened
The tube and the rush hour, the papers for sale
They arrive at the office and open their mail

Meanwhile, the school bus arrives at the gate
The kids disembark quickly, so as not to be late
Armed with their school bags and mobile phones
Discussing the soaps they watched last night at home

The parents with babies are staying at home
And buying their homes with discounted loans
As soon as their babies reach kindergarten age
They're off to work and freed from their cage

It's the end of the day and families arrive home
To microwave dinners and amplified tones
From Dolby surround and video laughs
The art of conversation is a thing of the past.

Clive Atkins

Look At The Moon

Look at the moon child, look at the moon.
See how its clear face pierces the gloom.
Don't let the darkness hamper your feet.
Don't be afraid of the things you can't see,
Look at the moon child, look at the moon.

Look at the moon child, look at the moon.
As it rides there in space, so glorious and bright.
So proud of its beauty, tho' black is the night.
Look at the moon.

Hold your head high, let your face feel its ray.
Light that will fade with the coming of day.
A spiritual light that we all have to share.
Look at the moon child, look at the moon.

The moon is a beacon, gentle but strong.
It is distant, mysterious, virginal, pure.
It links day to day with its comforting light.
We know God is there, even tho' it is night.
Sometimes clouds try to hide it but it will endure.
Stand proud. Be humble.
Look at the moon.

Jean Charman

SECRET WORLD

The beach is a world of its own,
It's a beautiful place to be,
After its beauty has been shown,
It's left all for me.

My beach talks a language that only it knows,
Although I know it too well,
The sea gives the beach its sparkly clothes
Its secret it's not willing to tell.

When the holidaymakers clear out,
The sea creatures scuttle away,
Then I can run, play and shout,
The magic renews every day.

The last boat glides by,
I catch a chill,
And say goodbye.
Then I walk up the long verdant hill.

Leni Freeman (10)

THE POSTMAN

He brings letters and bills
In wind and in rain
In snow and sleet
In darkness and in light.
Dogs are always a danger
Their bite but not their bark.
In time you learn the names
Of most within your round
And sometimes people stop and say
'Good morning Postman!'
All too often he's taken for granted
But he can never be supplanted.

Henry Rayner

To Veronica

Scattered o'er the horizon, surging t'ward the sky
Stands a city of ghostly pallor - where the sleepers silently lie.
'Tis where my love was sleeping, but now she can be found -
In a formless beauty creeping - above that sacred ground.

A wreath of tangled pansies - lay scattered upon her bed,
And the angels came to mourn - when the ritual was read.
A requiem so sweetly sung - on that final day -
Upon my memory heavy hung - until they flew away!

Here I whispered her sweet name - in a mournful lullaby,
And when I whispered it again - I heard a lowly sigh.
'Go up to God,' I said, 'ye must! Stay not thee here behind!
For soon thy beauty shall be dust - of the ill-begotten kind!'

Here I whispered her sweet name, but an echo dids't reply
And when I whispered it again - I heard a lowly sigh,
And through the dreary, dreamy rain, I saw a shapeless form.
'Go up to God and heavenly fane, beyond the gathering storm!'

Paul Allen Hill

WET PLAY

Dinner ladies hate wet play.
It makes an hour seem like a day.
In the hall there's so much noise
'Please quieten down you girls and boys.
Will you sit properly on your chair?'
'Ben don't put jelly in Emma's hair.'
Back in the classroom the toys are out
'Will you please not scream and shout!'
Paper, crayons all over the floor.
'Who's that escaping through the door?'
Lego, jigsaws, 'Who threw that?'
A book goes flying across the mat.
'David's got my coat, it's new.'
'Please Miss, can I go to the loo?'
'Let's all sit down, I'll read a story.'
'Oh yes, read the one that's gory!'
There's the bell, my duty's done
Now I'm off to see my mum.
Rain, rain please go away,
Dinner ladies hate wet play.

Diane King

INSIDE RAPE

My hands are tied with bloodied rope
My eyes are not my own
Those finger painted rings of hope
Were things I should have shown
Instead I chose to scar myself
With dead clowns in my mind
And tear out colours from my eyes
To let myself go blind

I'll scratch the door of my own pain
'Til no more wood is seen
Then wait to hear the rusted chain
Wrap round my only dream
Of ending all this black inside
And adding other shades
But I can't find the rainbow
And I'm running out of days

I've taken all the clocks apart
To give myself more time
So I can work out where to start
This painting in my mind
I found a brush to add my ink
Now all I need's a knife
To cut the hate I'm feeling
And begin a whole new life.

Sarah Murphy

BRITAIN'S ANSWER

Hitler shouted, raved, then made his boast,
'Bomb England! and make her roast'.
The British lion, fresh from his lair,
With extra wings to beat the air,
Has called the Nazi eagle's leader's dare.

'Bomber command!' over Berlin
Grit and sand, versus city of sin,
Hamburg and Frankfurt straffed and sandwiched,
With concentrated bombing, hot as mustard,
No wonder Hitler's feeling flustered.

Now the RAF's photographs have shown,
The devastation of Cologne,
Emden, blasted flat, hemmed in
With only the essence left of Essen,
We'll soon be rid of this German cancer,
Now they know, 'Britain's answer'.

Alfred Smirk

A LITTLE BIT SANE

Hell is burning for the evil ones.

It is for those that leave the weak to die
And leave the lonely ones to cry.

It is for the ones who hurt and deceive.
It is for those who do not believe
That everyone deserves the right
To live in peace and never fight.

Hell is for the ones who spoil themselves
With things they do not need,
With too much money while others go poor
Their lives mean nothing to me.

I would rather work for the gifts that I get
I can be happy in a life free of regret.
Be free from the fear of an eternity of pain
Just by being a little bit sane.

Carolyn Bainbridge

No

In the dark, inside my head
I lie upon my bleeding bed
Severed by a bitter blow
With the little word of 'no'

No surprise, it is my fate
Hook and line I took the bait
Just one word, each single letter
Couldn't express my life much better

I accept without much grace
The coldness of refusal's face
Play the game and never show
The feeling left when hearing no

So many times I've heard this song
I'm favoured odds - but still I'm wrong
Sometimes I think I've won this game
To find the outcome is the same

Bitterness - it runs so deep
No wonder that my mind can't sleep
Tortured pains of tears run dry
Bring daylight smiles that see me . . . sigh.

K Bryan

A LAST FAREWELL
(For Sue and Vic,
on the tragic, untimely death of their only son Philip)

Thank you for the life you gave me
Thank you for the love that made me
Thank you for the womb that bore me
Thank you both for watching o'er me
Thank you for the way you raised me
Thank you every time you praised me
Thank you when you had to scold me
Thank you when your arms enfold me
Thank you every time you kissed me
Thank you for the way you miss me
Thank you for the life you gave me.

Cliffe Lambert

DIRTY LINEN

Pitter-patter, it's raining again
Been kicking my shoes and I'm dirty and stained
Daddy's gonna moan, Mama's gonna nag
More dirty laundry for her linen bag.

Boys will be boys, girls will be girls
Why must I be the one with all the curls
Don't be late home from school
You know the score, you know the rules.

One more term then I'm out of school
I knew the score but broke all the rules
Don't want to end up on the dole
Gonna buy me some tools, let the good times roll.

Don't be playing out till late
Don't be getting in such a state
Because Daddy will moan, Mama will nag
More dirty laundry for her linen bag.

Michael Fennell

WEE BUMBLEBEES

Wee bumblebees
Scraped all their knees
Crashed into roses
Bashed all their noses
Wee bumblebees

Wee butterflies
Up in the skies
Flutter on the flowers
For hours and hours
Wee butterflies

Wee ladybirds
Lost for words
Hums a wee tune
And smiles at the moon
Wee ladybirds

Wee earwigs
Chased all the pigs
All around the farm
And in the stinky barn
Wee earwigs

Wee furry bats
Wearing funny hats
Hiding in the rocks
Wearing purple socks
Wee furry bats

Wee white mice
Sugar and spice
Took all the cheese
And never said, 'Please'
Wee white mice.

Eleanor Morgan

A REJECTION

Rejection is a painful word,
Something completely, utterly absurd,
A terrible state to find yourself,
Such heartache, and tainted wealth.

Crumbs of life are offered you,
Instead of wonders warm and true,
You feel downtrodden, down at heel,
Fortunes - pathway you didn't steal.

Always someone else experiencing the best,
You are simply down, feeling depressed,
Others always get the upperhand,
Leaving you feeling without command.

Sorrow in your heart you were never received,
Deluged and worn into solitude,
Never give up, you may reign one day,
Rejection a terrible price to pay.

Denise Hackett

STREET LAMPS

Six lamps in a row.
Dark winter's chill, another new low,
Wet, hazy head, wet hazy glow,
English evening running slow,
Head to paper running slow,
Damp cigarette, damp hazy glow,
Another new season, another new low
For street lamps in a row.

Pablo Vander Suilé

FOREVER I'M WITH YOU
(Dedicated to Tina Wahlin)

Don't stand at my grave weeping
For I not lay there sleeping
I did not die
I'm every newborn baby's cry
I'm every bird flying so high
I'm the brightest star in the black sky
I'm the hardest day you got by
I'm the warm sun's rays
And long, cold winter days
I'm the air you breathe
And every dream you conceive
I'm the wave crashing on the shore
And the crack in every wood floor
I'm the tranquillity you never saw
And every wish you wished for
I'm the greenest grass you've seen
And nicest place you've been
I'm the warm summer's breeze
And long cold winter's freeze
I'm the spring's blossoming trees
And autumn's dying leaves
I'm the strongest feeling you believe
And falsest idea you've conceived
I'm watching over you constantly,
In your heart I'll always be,
Look in your minds to see me, living eternally free
Memories to keep, so my spirit never sleeps
Although my body lies deep, I did not die, I do not sleep
Wipe the tears, don't cry, hold your head up high
I'm the infinite sky so blue, together anything we can do
Deep in your veins I flow through, *forever I'm with you.*

Richard Fiford

I AM FREE

Freedom lives within the mind
Not in the human shell
Many chained and tortured
Have learnt to weave the spell

Through the pain and suffering
The light within them burns
Then just like a lighthouse
Around the land it turns

Those who would ignore it
Must ponder on their stance
Remember in the future
You joined the despot dance

Every death that happens
Will lie there at your door
Speak against the tyranny
And feel your spirits soar

Every man's your brother
And for him you must speak
If tyrants sit in power
They will exploit the weak

Religion and politics
Both of the left and right
Will use their armed forces
To keep you from the light

Stand against oppression
Fight for a better world
Keep yourself an open mind
Find the truth unfurled

Ignore all the rhetoric
Use your eyes to see
Battle all injustice
Then you will be free.

Dagworth Orville Charters

FRIENDS

In these days of war and strife
We have to face the facts of life
Our foes are many, friends are few
So it is up to me and you
To value friendship very high,
For it is on them that we rely,
For that kindly word, and a cheerful smile
To help to make things seem worthwhile.
So my friends, just bear in mind,
Friends are very hard to find
Cling to them where e'er you roam
For without friends, you stand alone.

Marjorie Garrett

A Child's Ode To Valentine's Day

Mummy and Daddy I love you so
But there is something I would like to know!
Why do all the ladies pine
For this lover Valentine?
He turns up only once a year
To whisper sweet words in their ear!
Then he's gone and no one knows
Where he's from and where he goes.
They say he's from enchanted lands,
Which you can reach by holding hands
And being nice to one another.
You'll be a lovely dad and mother!

A B McIlquham

UNTITLED

I pulled into the drive with the shopping
And dumped all the bags in the hall
It was then that I noticed the letter
It was pinned to the board on the wall

It told me that you'd met another
You said you would like to be free
You told me that you would be leaving
The dog and the children and me

You said you were terribly sorry
Hoped I wouldn't think you a louse
You wrote that there would be some money
When I sold the car and the house

I flew up the stairs in a panic
Just couldn't take in the bad news
The doors to your wardrobe were open
You'd taken your clothes and your shoes

Whatever would I tell the children
My Harri, my Charlie, my Jack.
Your daddy's decided to leave us.
He's gone and he's not coming back

We cried and we cried for a fortnight
Then I said, 'We've got to make plans
We'll sell up the house and possessions
And go where there's sun, sea and sand.'

Now eighteen months on we are happy
We've got a great house by the sea
And new friends coming round for a 'bar b'
We've come to Australia, 'yippee'!

Jo Partner

AUTUMN DAYS

Leaves are curling and turning gold.
Jack Frost's been, so it must be cold.
Conkers swelling, ready to drop.
Cutting the grass - well that can now stop.
Empty the pots with all the dead flowers.
The forecast said we shall get some showers.

No more butterflies, no more bees.
No more weeding on bended knees.
Barbecue cleaned, won't need it again.
Decking painted and ready for rain.
Gutters checked, all are clear.
We don't want overflows, coming from here.

Nights draw in and fires are lit.
Huddled around in armchairs we sit.
Cuddled up, all cosy and snug.
Even the dog is asleep on the rug.
With a great big yawn, we climb the stairs.
A kiss goodnight, and say our prayers.

Genevieve Powell

CARNAGE

I really don't know what to do,
The sky that was once blue,
Is now covered up with smoke,
In one awful stroke.

The fate of so many lives,
As the first of the planes dives.
No one could know what it could do,
Except the demented few,

Who used religion for their own goal,
To increase the horrible and senseless death toll.
Little did they, the people know,
That it was their time, there was nowhere else for them to go.

Screaming, yelling and falling about,
This was nothing short of a bloody rout.
The twisted face, broken bones.
Hurtling down towards the paving stones.

The burning buildings finally caving in,
The explosions, *oh God,* what a din.
What a loss of human life,
Someone's husband, someone's wife.

Never will they ever enjoy what they once had,
This bloody day, this disgusting day is nothing but sad,
Sad and sad.
We must all unite on this sorrowful day,
To keep evil at bay.

God does not say *kill in my name*
It's only the sad individuals who are to blame.
Who use religion to divide,
We are but one, there can be no one side.

Mohammed Farooq

A Tribute To A Perfect Lady

Let's not forget the years of pain,
Life must go on, though sometimes in vain,
A perfect example was the Queen Mum
And as she got older, her life became fun.

But sadly the way of life was meant to be,
Passing away into tranquillity
And as you remember her in so many ways,
Long before my time she brought strength to save.

The ones she never forgot were in her mind,
The early years she had were such a lot of the hurtful kind,
But like all the war years, she stood proud you see
And like so many that fought in years gone by
To survive both you and me.

I will always remember her by,
The gentle smile that brought tears to the eye,
The gentle reflection on all of her life,
Was maybe the fact she had great strife.

But a kinder person you would never find
And she tried to teach others, the gentle way to be kind,
Her love of life she never did let down
And may I now pay this tribute from Kendal's clown.

But the sad clown always was a loser, you see
And as I look back over years of what was meant to be,
To see a special person in a very special way,
I now am saying have some respect and cast a thought and pray.

Barbara Holme

PRISYNDROME

The four grey walls that surround me,
The cracked ceiling that serves as my roof
The bars at my doors and my windows,
All designed to be escape-proof.
Can you on the outside imagine
Being trapped in a room so designed
To create all the symptoms of panic,
Have you ever been so confined?

The answer, my friend, is yes you are,
Though not physically I agree
For one of the first things one learns inside
Is to let the mind roam free
Only then can you see how trapped you are,
Enmeshed in your own private webs
Invisible limiting boundaries,
A vortex through which time ebbs.

Your body is free, your mind is trapped,
Your confinement differs from mine
I can lay on my bunk and close my eyes
And imagine the most divine
I can fly to the moon in a spacecraft
Or go yachting at Cowes for a week
Climb mountains in the Andes
And look down from the highest peak.

It's all in my mind and I know it,
My body has nowhere to roam
But what about you on the outside,
With your bodies trapped in your home?
The four brick walls that surround you,
The bright ceiling that serves as your roof
No bars at the doors or the windows,
But like mine it's still escape-proof.

There's no way of escaping the payments,
The mortgage, the rates or the rent
There's always a harassing problem to solve
And remain solvent
There is a way to escape of course,
Pay nothing! Just like me
Come join us inside, out of the way
And let your minds roam free!

R D Lambourne

THE ROCKING CHAIR

Rocking . . . backward, forward, backward:
Crocheted, patchwork shawl drawn tight.
Thinking . . . backward, forward, backward;
Grandfather cloth tick-tocks the night.

Soot-black kettle hangs to simmer . . .
Long, brass poker stirs the coal;
Katie's eyes are growing dimmer . . .
Pulls more tight her shawl of wool.
Shining brass winks in the firelight . . .
Sparking thoughts of long-lost days;
Days when Kate was young and bright . . .
And beautiful with winning ways.

Secret smile now shapes worn lips . . .
Laughter brightens clouded eyes;
Sweet memories of seaside trips,
When 'twas thought 'Folly to be wise'.
Rowing boat on the park lake . . .
Building castles in the sand;
Nights of Charleston . . . ah! First date . . .
Back row pictures, holding hands.

Rocking . . . backward, forward, backward;
Crocheted, patchwork shawl drawn tight.
Thinking . . . backward, forward, backward;
Grandfather clock tick-tocks the night.

Black market tins of Irish stew . . .
Planes and bombs and air-raid shelter;
Smart uniform of air-force blue . . .
Heart turned over, helter-skelter.
No wedding bells or special leave . . .
Vows exchanged 'twixt bombing raids;
Stark telegram! Time to grieve . . .
Memories which will never fade.

Fierce snow lashing at the casement,
Clinging fast to each small pane.
More coal needed from the basement . . .
Katie reaches for her cane.
Embers crumbling . . . fire falling . . .
Kettle humming, swinging slow.
Alas, no one can hear Kate calling
As she slips on frozen snow . . .

Slipping . . . backward, forward, down;
Crocheted, patchwork shawl drawn tight.
Katie whispers silent moan . . .
Grandfather clock tick-tocks the night.

Doris Sproston

UNTITLED

From the debate
to the States
to the firing squad
just a big fat wad
of brains.
Now it rains
all red
because of the bloodshed.
So young
yet so serious
I'm not delirious.
Just mixed up
like a young pup.
It's so grimy
yet I'm still rhyming
all that fire and passion
like the waves crashin'
all this on the street
but I'm still making beats
in my head
full of lead.

Laura Hughes (15)

WHY?

I miss the sound of the opening door
The tread of your footsteps on the floor
A smile in your eyes, the warmth of your breath
All this I miss so much since you left
Why did you leave, I don't understand
I do so miss the touch of your hand
You went away and I stand and cry
Alone am I now, left to ask, why?

George Hebdon

WOMEN

Complicated are the lives of women,
Their minds are drowning as their hearts are swimming
The game consists of loss and gain,
Not to suffer intolerable pain.
The woman has one ambition in life,
To succeed through all her strife,
Battling against the challenges thrown
A woman's emotions are easily shown.
The continuation of the human race,
. . . Women take in their own pace.
This is the version that has been told -
Women can be strong and women can be bold!
The time is now to achieve your goal,
Multiply your spirit and apply your soul!
Negative things happen for a reason - they make you strong
When nothing else is left, all hope isn't gone
So if you take this light-heartedly,
Look and see there's plenty of me . . . women!

Janette Dann

REVELATIONS

Came the American pimping Jehovah without pity,
Importing revelations upon England's timeworn city;
Enunciating the call for liberty while compelling sacrifice,
Intoned this benighted captain from a material enterprise.
Denouncing with ridicule the opposing voice of democracy,
Carving gravestones which partition, a cornered world despairing;
O' wise independent cynics, discourage such foolish hypocrisy
For these are virtuous reasons to protest the cross, we're baring.
How every battle and smoke screen are blindly cursed and plain,
Securing the blackest of gold by which harmony was eagerly slain;
Trapped is every soul, between the causes of a godless Western feast,
In addition to the cruel effectual intolerance, of a murderous
                                                    Middle East.
Where each demon of commerce manages to cause, alarm;
Paying for the chequered history of ever bitter pawn of Islam.
America now surely yearns respect through serenity,
To all peaceful citizens! Rebuke the acts of tyranny.

William Shaun Milligan

THE MOUNTAINEER

Man is born - achievements be his quest.
Until his cup be filled he cannot be at rest.
Yon lofty slopes with jagged edge reaching to the sky;
A challenge left by nature to top its mast so high.

Complete with pickaxe, rings and rope, he goes his merry way,
To test limited endurance as Mother Nature would say.
Like the building of a tower, it's finished at the point;
Step by step from foundation measured by each joint.

Slippery slopes, sheer precipice, footholds must be made
Mistakes if there be any, all hope will soon fade.
Limbs are aching, body shaking, mind says turn back;
A goal was set, it must be reached, willpower he mustn't lack.

At last the peak be closer, hope upon breast,
A last great surge of the body then a well-earned rest.
From this great height he peers around - everything looks so small.
Great nations, vast land, he feels he owns them all.

John McDonald

NAN

I close my eyes and see your face that smile that would have been,
Then I think about that certain smell of soap upon your skin.
And it warms my heart and makes me smile each time I think of you,
So whenever I am feeling down I know just what to do.

I think of all the times we've had, the fun that you would make.
Like dancing round your living room and cakes that we would bake.
You helped raise us from childhood; you've seen how we have grown
And led us to our own lives with the love that you have shown.

We know that you are here with us, that you're by our sides today,
Watching us your family, as we express our sad dismay.
We hope that you are happy and don't feel any badness,
In this time that we all grieve and feel extraordinary sadness.

You used to say that you believed a monk watched over you,
Well I hope that you are with him now and what you believed is true.
I'm glad that I got to say goodbye, to have given you a final kiss,
As your beauty and such special ways I will always surely miss.

Though you've departed from this world our love will never die,
And even though it hurts inside we know we mustn't cry.
'Cause you have gone to a better place, somewhere that you can rest,
And we would like for you to know, that you'll always be the best.

Ricky Cairns

REALISATION OF A NEW LIFE

I'm not sure where it all began,
life's pace just quickened up to a run.
No real chance to catch my breath,
or even think of my inevitable death.

Sliding down that slippery slope
I had street knowledge, no ray of hope.
From a self-centred world I was miles apart,
how could I dream of a clean, fresh start?

All the pain and hurt I've caused
while tightly gripped in an addict's claws.
It seemed like nothing at the time,
but now I know I was out of line.

It went from parties in fun and jest,
casual using like all the rest,
but somewhere and somehow along the line
it became impossible to decline.

My life had taken on a whole new meaning,
one devoid of thought and feeling.
A one-track mind . . . living a lie . . .
all I cared about was chasing the buzz
of that first real high.

One day I stopped and I took a look,
I'd lost direction, I was really hooked.
I sat myself down and thought for a while
how destructive was my lifestyle?
all misplaced thoughts, real strong denial.
I'd had too much of putting my life on trial.

So I sat and worked it through,
the word rehab was my clue.
Live or die, my own debts were due.

I started it off, I sparked the light,
this beacon now guides me
through my fight.

From a life of dread and fear,
comes one in which is crystal clear,
of which direction I'm heading in,
where I don't need chemicals - they are a sin.

Ben Cutler

LIFE

We are but a grain of sand,
Running free in no-man's-land,
What our heart desires our soul doesn't need,
We are living amongst stress and greed,
We continually search but we don't know what for,
Could it be that there is no more!

We all at stages want to shout,
'Please tell me what life is all about!'
One day when we cross to the great Divine,
He will know what we have been doing all this time,
Preparing us for another way,
But until then we must live each day,
So go and enjoy your every hour,
Life is a gift from a great power.

Linda Redelinghuys

THE SILENT INTRUDER

The dark, dismal December day,
Gave life to the shadowed intruder that had nothing to say,
And yet, my life would change forever,
Cos it was impossible to sever,
This intruder from my thoughts.

The intruder worked hard day and night,
And assumed it had the right
To control my senses and my thoughts,
Causing trauma of all sorts
For family, friends and acquaintances too,
But how, or what, could be done,
To extinguish this intruder and make it gone
From existence.

Men of knowledge expected to win,
This challenge,
To extinguish this intruder from within,
But,
Alas, time reared its ugly head,
The intruder's tentacles began to spread,
The tumour enveloped my head,
I existed no more,
And the intruder became extinct.

H S Burn

TAWE (RIVER)

In lonely hills, my story starts
The likeness of a new-born calf.
A spring evolves through God's own might
Silent journey through the night

Ancient legend and bards alike
Worship him who has such might
The story goes that he was strong
Gains respect from threatening throng

Like a path that has no end
The water flows with human trend
Right or wrong it holds its course
Viking wind shows no remorse

Through moon and sun she wanders on
Like mighty folk who do so wrong
Back on course her goal in sight
Celtic cross has such might

Noble knight will don her name
In castle high, whence he came
Clerics claim a foreign title
Tawe now has Celtic bridle

Meeting places and temples stand
Bonded mother gives a hand
Greater springs wait in court
Jesus' message, food for thought.

Sampson

STALKER

At your window looking in
On their face a hint of sin
They're watching every move you make
Your privacy they're bound to take
They follow you everywhere you go
Strangely, you don't even know
When you're walking down the street
Behind you hear the sound of feet
Take a look if you dare
You turn around there's no one there

They find the best place to hide
To watch you home and go inside
If you knew they'd cause you stress
Looking in when you undress
Over you they have strange power
They see you when you take a shower
From behind a privet hedge they peep
They're even there when you're asleep
It's much worse when you're aware
Knowing that a psycho's there

They turn your life upside down
You're too scared to go to town
You don't know if they'll make a move
The fact they're there is hard to prove
You're the one who has to pay
Until they're caught and locked away
Your life's becoming a living hell
Your home has turned into a cell
Don't give in and let them win
Phone the police to take them in.

Neil Warren

SATAN'S BREW
(Dedicated to the miners of Castle Hill Colliery in Scotland)

The heavy fall of highland rain
Each drop of morning dew,
Had helped to cause the fear and pain,
And make that devil's brew.
The farmer's field awash with mud as Satan sat there drinking,
Death lay concealed, beneath that field, as slowly it was sinking.

Perhaps a gentle trickle and then a mighty roar,
As tons and tons of peat and mud rushed to that old mine floor.
A moment felt in fear with dread, the panic there was plenty.
While some were living, some were dead and the devil's bowl
was empty.

For five long days and longer nights, each man and boy would toil,
Some would try to block the hole, with trees and straw and soil,
But still the ticking of the clock and still the rain was dripping,
And still his cruel laughter, as Satan kept on sipping.

With flesh and bone they hacked the stone that held their kith and kin,
As one by one they took their turn to drive a roadway in,
Each father at his brother's side, or with his brother's son,
The limestone, shale, the stone and coal, they moved it ton by ton.

Young Jim was there with his pick in hand, each blow a
pounding thrust,
A blast of air, his fearful stare, into the cloud of dust.
'I'm through,' young Jimmy whispered, *'I'm through!'* he cried
out loud,
And cheers came from the darkness as Jim stood in that cloud.

One hundred men survived that day, one hundred men were saved,
But thirteen men were dead and gone, had met muddy grave,
Those thirteen granite gravestones, on 'Knochsinnoch's' grassy slope,
While trapped within, their kith and king, had never given up hope.

Fifty years have been and gone, two score years and ten,
No more a mine on Castle Hill, no more the mining men,
But still the hole at Satan's bowl and still the widows' tears,
And still the petals on the graves, not faded with the years.

C Muter

NEW BEGINNINGS

Spring is coming, I know that to be so.
I have seen the dainty snowdrops peeping through the snow.
I have seen the gaudy crocuses colouring the lawns.
I have heard the birds awakening in the earlier dawns.
The blackbirds are parading with feathers black as jet,
Prancing before the dowdy hens which recently they met.
There are daffodils in bud amid their spear-shaped leaves.
There are hosts of chirpy sparrows nesting in the eaves.
There is blossom on the currant bush and flowering cherry too,
And gardeners nodding wisely and saying what's to do.
The days are getting longer, the sun is warmer too,
I love this silly season where everything is new.

Jan Coverdale

The Wonders Around Us

Colourful rainbow high in the sky
After the storm has passed by
Puddles of rain adorn the lanes
Little raindrops on the windowpanes
As you sit on a gate or stile
Look around and see for miles.

Take in the clean fresh air
Feel how marvellous it is to be there
See buttercups all scattered around,
As the sun peeps from behind the clouds
Casting sunshine all over the fields
As the cows go plodding home with their yield.

Little rabbits nibbling and scampering around
Beneath the outstretched leafy boughs
With little oak leaves glistening anew
Singing and twittering birds hidden from view
So when you feel there is strife
Treasure these wonderful things in life.

Rita Evans

FUN FOR THE WEALTHY!

As she forages through deep greenery
In the cold and windy chill of the dawn
Looking for scraps or easy prey,
Shivering, frightened, feeling very forlorn.

Serena, a beautiful vixen, was tragically widowed
Less than one week ago,
Her proud partner savaged by dogs,
Filling her heart with immeasurable woe.

Deep in woodland by a scenic brook,
Icy water tricking down heather-clad rocks,
Unspoilt by man, hidden away,
This is the 'Mayfair' of woodland to the fortunate fox.

Four young cubs venture from the warmth of their den,
Hunger pangs causing distress,
The usual provider of all food is no more;
Mother exhausted under increasing duress.

Serena returns with the scraps, devoured in seconds
By the starving, ungrateful brood,
Reflecting on the days when her handsome red warrior
Provided all of the food.

The vixen is weakening; sleek red coat turns muddy brown,
Much prominence of bone.
The idyllic lifestyle has been shattered,
Now survival the instinct, terrified and alone.

What had happened to her hero on that fateful day
When he set out never to return?
Serena knows well of his savage final fate,
Reflection making her stomach churn.

Hunting to provide for those hungry young cubs
He was happy and proud of his lot,
The cry of distant hounds, a bugle sounded,
A distant echo once heard and never forgot.

His scent had been discovered, his life was on the edge;
He had to outrun the hound,
Blind panic mixed with the cunning of the fox,
Heart pounding he covered the ground.

Knowing his terrain intimately well,
His mind began racing ahead as he surged forth,
Eyes bulging, limbs aching, hounds gaining,
He knew of a haven a mile further north.

Inspired by Serena, the light of his life,
Exhausted, he spotted the golden field of corn,
Outrunning his foe over many hard miles,
Finding safety in the den where he was born.

Muscles contracting, cramping, frozen in time,
Terror now mixed with a desire to survive,
Hearing digging above him, trapped in his den,
A desperate feeling he wouldn't get out alive.

Ripped from his haven, hounds bayed for his blood
And huntsman who led them did too,
Torn limb from limb, chilling screams fill the air,
Celebrations as all the horns blew.

Strewn in mud, his tail butchered off,
Providing a trophy for champions of their sport.
Once a sleek hunter, Serena's king of their 'Woodland Heaven'
Had fatally been caught.

The cubs ever hungry, Serena struggles to cope
With the pressure to keep them all healthy,
Horror fills her thoughts as she reflects on her day,
Her 'love' provided 'fun for the wealthy!'

David A Johnson

SHELLEY THE JELLY BEAR

Shelley was a special bear, not like you and me
Shelley was a special bear as anyone could see
All the other bears around her knew her from the telly
For unlike the other bears, she was made of jelly

Shelley was the sweetest bear that you could wish to meet
Jellicious from her pretty head down to her jelly feet
She loved to lick her fingers and her tiny little toes
'Cause jelly is so tasty as everybody knows

Some days she tasted of strawberries and other days of peach
Some days of ripe bananas the ones you cannot reach
Some days she tasted of grapefruit and other days of lemon
Her friends liked it best when she tasted of watermelon

Shelley was a jelly bear so special as you can see
Shelley was a jelly bear not like you and me
But jelly doesn't last forever, it melts in the sun
And Shelley didn't like that, it wasn't much fun

Then one day came a magic man with a wand and spell
He asked Shelley if she had a wish, she had he could tell
'I want to be like other bears that's all I want for me'
The magic man then tapped his wand and counted up to three

Shelley closed her eyes and wished with all her heart
She could feel something happening it gave her such a start
She opened her eyes because she couldn't wait anymore
She took a deep breath and headed for the door

Shelley looked around her and saw to her delight
The sun shining brightly, not a star in sight
Shelley was so happy she gave a mighty roar
For Shelley the jelly bear wasn't jelly anymore

M Hazlehurst

TAKE TIME

This wonderful world is full of surprises
Full moons, stars and glorious sunrises
Azure seas and golden beaches with seashells
Jungles, woods, forests and dells
Vast oceans, great lakes and lagoons.
Downpours, sun showers and warm monsoons
Mountains so high, they are capped with snow
Valley so fertile flowering down below
Rivers that run so fast and crystal clear
Salmon that swim up and jump over the weir.
Deserts, tundras, dunes and wasteland places
They all have a beauty and some with oasis.
The pole with its icebergs and glaciers glisten
It's so vast, if you shout, there's no one to listen
Great spectacles created for us to explore
If only, we would stop, take time, and see more.

Denis Browne

WHEN THE MIST HAS CLEARED

When the mist has cleared and the sun is shining through
I look up to the Lord above and see you smiling too
The warm glow, of peace and serenity
The feeling of being at ease
As the sun lays down its warmth to us breaking through the trees

In all its glory sending us, the warmth sent from your heart
Strengthening each other's love since we were forced apart
Remembering the memories of love, the laugh, the pain
Dancing barefoot in the snow and lying in the rain

Together, forever, we'll never be apart
Inside my chest is burning 'sunburn' of the heart

For when the mist has cleared and the sun is shining through
I look up to the Lord above and see I'm smiling too.

Shaun Maccoy

THAT CHRISTMAS FEELING

Snow falls; it's cold, so cold.
Someone to cuddle, someone to hold.
Logs in the hole blazing with fire,
Mince pies on a plate for your desire.
Gifts on the floor for under the tree,
Turkey in the oven, for you and me.
Mistletoe hanging for where to be kissed,
A Christmas to remember, not to be missed.

Lindsay Clarke

JACK FROST

Come closer and listen and I'll tell you a tale
About a Mr Jack Frost and his naughty wee snail.
They lived in a land where the sun shone all day,
And flowers would bloom in the most fabulous way.
Now Jack and his snail were a mischievous pair,
They did naughty things, they just didn't care.
It was them that pushed Humpty and caused him to fall,
They tormented Tom Thumb just because he was small.
They hid all the sheep that belonged to Bo Peep,
But behaviour like this brought them trouble so deep.
News of their deeds soon spread far and wide,
So Jack and his snail decided to hide.
The Queen she got angry at the things they had done
And decided to put an end to their fun.
She banished the pair to a land of snow and ice,
Because behaving like that just wasn't nice.
The snail he was sorry so the Queen let him go,
'Cause a snail he would die in a land full of snow.
But naughty young Jack he just didn't care,
'Cause mischief he knew he could do anywhere.
So when you look out your window on a cold winter's day,
You know Mr Frost has been past your way,
'Cause the pavements all glisten and the cars are all ice,
I know what you're thinking, it all looks so nice,
But frost can be slippy, take care you don't fall,
On the cold winter mornings when Jack comes to call.

Maureen Moffat

SPAIN

Lounging on my balcony
I gaze out at the glorious sea
Myriad colours green and blue
Sparkle just like the morning dew

White horses riding on the sea
Waves crash in relentlessly
Fishing boats go out at night
Catching fish with all their might

Sailing boats are out at sea
White sails gleaming out at me
Mountains in the distance lie
Snow-capped peaks both low and high

Lovely sunsets o'er the sea
Bring peace and pure tranquillity
The glories of the setting sun
Tell me that the day is done

Damas de Noche in the park
Wondrous smell when it gets dark
I love the jacaranda tree
The blossom's beautiful to see

Geraniums on the balconies grow
Winter too - in glorious flow
When at work I'm feeling low
Spain is where I long to go

Eileen Green

TUFFY

Tuffy has been through a lot in his life,
Like when he was made to go under the knife.
He stayed at the vet during the night
And we picked him up in the morning light.
Tuffy has always been up to no good,
From escaping his cage whenever he could.
He looks so sweet with his eyes open wide,
They make him shine with lots of pride.
Tuffy is always making me smile,
Like when he looks at me for a while.
I love to spoil him at every chance,
And all he does is give me a glance.
Tuffy is like a small teddy bear,
Soft and cuddly yet always aware.
He is very good at climbing the stairs,
And he is always walking right off the chair.
Tuffy is always wanting a treat
And it's hard to say no because he's so sweet.
He won't give in to getting his way,
No matter the cost we'll have to pay.
I love to spend time with him every day,
Because I don't care what people might say.
Tuffy will insist on climbing his bars,
Sometimes I think he's aiming for Mars.
Tuffy will always be my boy,
Who is always bringing me lots of joy.
So no matter what mischief he might get up to,
I'll always love him 'cause that's what I do!

Sarah Hollingsworth (11)

Man In My Mind

I often ponder and imagine his face,
and in my mind I feel his embrace.
His face changes from time to time,
as my dialogue fills his mime.
My wishful and heightened emotional state
cannot be dismissed, as I still wait
for this beautiful enigmatic king,
to present me with a sapphire ring
that will sparkle and glisten,
as I listen
to his adoring, yet passionate declaration
of his love that I'll reciprocate without hesitation.
This elusive love I yearn for,
I do not wish to wait my turn for.
I wish for it as soon as can be,
my intoxicating sweetheart come to me.
This love we'll share will be a mixture
for you in my heart will become a fixture,
of both contentment and burning passion,
you the love that I fashion.

Diana Doyle

THE DANCE OF LIFE

Everything begins at birth,
The day we arrive on Earth.
Picking our parents, a very wise thing to do
Then begins the dance of life without further ado.

Absorbing the rhythm of your mother's love,
Snuggling close as a good fitting glove.
You grow, become aware that you have a dad,
A benefit of which most families will be glad.

A few years on, you learn to move around,
Placing your feet firmly on the ground.
Then one day you realise the safeness of Earth's floor,
On the world of which we hope you will come to adore.

Every day that passes you learn much more,
The stronger you grow the more you wish to explore.
You learn to depend on those who love you,
In turn you must respond to love them too.

Leaving childhood and becoming a young adult,
You scan the big outside world for every fault.
Each day you wonder whether to stride ahead,
Or nervously dither, stand still, or be cautiously led.

Today, so many opportunities, all so inviting,
The dance of life for the young is so exciting.
Think positive and the world can be your oyster,
Think negative and be confined in your cloister.

The rhythm of life will urge you to mate,
Mother Nature will encourage you to keep that date.
It seems our world itself must perpetuate,
And its population must regenerate.

With a family in tow the dance goes on,
It gives you a purpose to work upon.
Its demands of your love, care and dedication,
And can bring you great sorrow or elation.

The family has matured and grown.
Your progeny in the nest now has flown.
Your partner and you can now enjoy a life of your own,
Your life in the future is set by the seeds you have sown.

Our new-found freedom allows us to stand and stare,
Thinking of how to enjoy our future life and where.
The end of the dance may be near or far,
Whatever, don't let despondency your future happiness mar.

The dance of life probably now has a slower beat,
Less challenges you will have to meet.
It's vital to retain your 'get up and go'
Keep Father Time at bay, that ever watchful so and so.

Rest and relax, enjoy the calm, the setting of the evening sun,
You have played your part in life, your span is nearly done.
If life was good, we hope it has been a happy one,
If it was hard, then blessed relief you will be happy to come.

The silence has told us the dance has stopped, it's run its race,
The dancer has retired with dignity and grace.
In death, your loved ones will honour you on bended knee,
Praying you go to Heaven for eternity.

We know not the purpose of the Dance of Life, unless it is to drive
us on,
With ups and downs, its disasters, its glories, new birth, ever moving
the world along.
Since this universe was created, its vitality has been driven
To respond to the Dance of Life, its beat and perpetual rhythm.

Terry Godwin

A HELPING HAND

Great Britain's not so great it seems
It used to be a land of dreams
Yet people from beyond our shore
They come knocking on our door
They must see something we can't see
To come so far and want to be
In this land we hold so dear
And now their lives are free of fear
We help them to forget their pain
I bet they think we are great again.

Kenneth Bailey

A SOLDIER'S LAST PRAYER

Abide with me, for it's not the glory,
Territory or province, tells the same story:
Protect your neighbour, for your lives do depend.
Stolen pride; the war's over, he's seen the end.
Remove that mark, an ill provoked laughter,
Creatures of the world are the same thereafter.

Clouded orchestra, wind howls a tuneful song.
That's my neighbour, walking through the streets beyond.
Desecrate buildings cloak the night sky.
Under the table, bottled whiskey's gone dry.
Star show reflections, conspiracy, intrigue.
Curtains have fallen, I'm drunk with fatigue.

Rose petals float like butterfly wings,
Across nameless streets, where my neighbour sings.
Redesigned buildings occupy an arch;
Paints white faces to those standing, ready to march.
'Wake up soldier, we're moving to Charlie'.
No more I scent illustrious fields of barley.

Wide-eyed knights have brotherhood and freedom.
Whispers to a neighbour, 'Walk by me to Eden'.
Darkness floods to the drumbeats' crescendo;
Not be Lucifer, not to insinuate, innuendo?
Wait at the door while the trumpets weep.
Hold me child, your father's asleep.

Life mystifies a delicate Swan Lake;
With spiral acquaintance, neighbours awake.
Too hot the eye that aligns my sight,
Neither night or day, succumbs painted light.
A game of cards, you pick them out; snap.
A still orphan cries tonight.

Stephen Alan Smith

SILENCE

There is healing in a silence like no other found on earth,
And if I sit alone awhile, I'll find it has true worth;
For it will give me peace of mind, from worries and all strife,
It will give me guidance to help me through my life.

I know that in the stillness, a strength will come to me,
Filling all my senses, freeing from anxiety.
From deep within my very soul, a voice will seem to speak,
Clearing all my muddled thoughts - I'll find that which I seek.

Take time for meditation, relax, do not be tense,
You'll find that in the quietness things will make more sense:
Just rest awhile in silence and you will surely find,
Tranquillity, a gentleness, and a peace of mind.

Beth Jones

IN MY ROOM

Last night there was someone who entered my room,
I could make out their image by the light of the moon.
The figure was standing just by the chair,
But my mind kept on telling me that it's not there.
The figure moved swiftly and then sat on the bed,
That's when all the bad thoughts entered my head.
Suddenly the room was filled with his voice,
I just laid there and froze, hey, I had no choice.
He started to tell me a story of old,
The feelings were so strong that I felt ice cold.
He went on to say that he'd been here before,
And how things had changed since the end of the war.
The name that was mentioned drew an uncanny resemblance
Of a man that I've heard of in war and remembrance.
Then out of the blue he broke into song,
And as I opened my eyes, the stranger was gone.
He never came back to the light of my room,
But I keep on thinking that he'll be somewhere soon.
For a world that keeps changing and the to and the fro,
I no longer ask myself, where do you go?

David R McNiece

HEROIN

Love me for the thing I am
Love me for what I do
I've got narcotic influences
I'm the drug to see you through

I'm the drug that causes all the deaths
The one they call the skag
Spending all your money
For my little tenner bag

You put the needle in your vein
And give yourself a jag
That's the way the heroin works
The one they call the skag

I'll take you into a faraway zone
When you're tired of life
I'm the reaper in my powder form
To free you from the norm

I'm the freedom you always wanted
when you take a hit
That little bag of powder
The one they call the kit

It's your own choice to dabble
And it's your own choice to play
So take me misled people
'Cause I am here to stay

So if you take this powder
You'll never dance and rave
You'll be happy for a short while
Then I'll send you to your grave.

Steven Wilson

MASKS

We are a minority
Beacons in the dark
Weighed down by the majority
None of us make a mark

Because we are true
We are shunned
How people like you
I am stunned

Your species flock
Like a herd of sheep
So many paths you block
And so I creep

Stick to the shadows
Don't stand out
Personality, say no
Always whisper, never shout

Soon I will explode
It's all happened before
I return down that road
Can't take anymore

What's your problem
With individuality
I'll never be like them
The disease won't get me

Tony Moran

MIRROR IN YOUR DARKNESS

I am the mirror in your darkness
The stars in the sky
A sweet caress
A butterfly as you pass by.

A whisper you never heard
A fleeting thought in your mind
Something you thought absurd
But were hoping to find.

I am the shadow behind you
The dreams in your sleep
I'll wipe your tears when you are blue
And comfort you when you weep.

I am the dew upon the grass
The dawn and rising sun
I am there when you laugh
And when the day is done.

Gill Green

Romantic Matt

Words cannot describe what you really mean to me
Next to you is the only place I really want to be
I hope there finally comes a time when all my dreams come true
When I'll be able to spend all my time side by side with you

I was going to send you flowers, it could have been a rose
Or maybe some chocolates or maybe who knows?
In the end I decided to send what really means the most
Which is all my love and kisses in this card through the post

I look out the window and the sea is so blue
It is really beautiful it reminds me of you
As I stand here listening to the waves upon the shore
It makes me wonder if I've ever felt this way before

Matt Burd

A STEP FURTHER

Night had fallen, as always will,
The view so different, tho' all so still.
Quiet and calm as life drifts by,
Knowing today I did but try.

Troubling times I left behind,
Ever present in my heart and mind.
I grew to believe and dared to trust,
The memory of which now turned to dust.

Tears I cried and wiped away,
I'm living my life, what's left to say?
Existence bears reason,
The direction different in every season.

Darkness brings fear,
The fear of a past so near.
The threat I feel again and again,
Still wondering why it causes me pain.

Nicola Goodison

WHY DON'T NO ONE NEED ME?

Why don't no one, 'like-love-want' or need me?
Apart from my family, which I see!
Is it because I am old, disabled and ugly . . . do I smell?
I wish people would be honest, and tell!
Please tell me why,
Before I cry!

People on the web like me, why not you?
As I am very honest, caring, reliable too!
some 'friends' used me, as they see me as their bank!
Maybe, sometimes, I am 'thick as a plank'!

I jump at the chance,
people ask flavours, which does make me 'munchance!' (Dumbstruck)
I would love to have real friends -
Flavours, parties, outings - which we attend!

One nice thing, my lovely daughter, help me to decide . . .
Not yet, to commit suicide!
So if you see me in the streets,
Ask me out and give me a treat!

Barry Ryan

TO BE ASHAMED

To never think of others
To never give a damn
To hide away in corners
To be ashamed
To be a man
To take all of the forest
To bring it to its knees
To pollute all of the rivers
To pollute all of the seas
To destroy the ozone layer
To poison all the air
To never think of others
To never really care

Greeny

FEELING OLD

At the moment I'm feeling old
As realities of life unfold.
My friends are dying all around,
I'm sitting here without a sound
Reflecting on the life I've had,
Sometimes good, sometimes bad.
Life has been quite good to me,
Love and kindness is all I see.
I have a good man, whom I love and trust.
Love and trust, I feel is a must.
My animals depend on me.
I hope there's a future for us to see.
Our children are doing well,
The grandchildren all cast their spell.
I've done my bit for family life,
I've seen them through without much strife.
Now I must try to relax and rest,
Knowing that I have done my best.

Lorna Flint

IF ONLY I HAD SPOKEN

I have been so stupid,
To ever let you go,
If only I had spoken,
And said, 'I love you so.'
What ever I was thinking,
The feelings I did hide,
If only I had spoken,
You would still be at my side.
Now two hearts are broken,
Forever and a day,
If only I had spoken,
This is what I'd say,
'I loved you then,
I love you now
Until the end of time.'
If only I had spoken
Your love would still be mine.

Peter Ramsden

UNTITLED

Spring arrives upon the fresh daybreak,
Removing the cold from our hearths.
Through the crack in the curtains,
Warmth enters into the room.

The ground begins to shed its cloak of night,
As daylight, slowly comes to the sky.
Exploding with a kaleidoscopic rainbow reflection,
Banishing neutrality from the realm.

Now is the time to shake off the frost,
For our coats are no longer required.
Wipe the sleep from our eyes,
The mists from our minds.

As the world, rises from slumber,
The acknowledgements for the things that matter,
Flow through the air in the breeze.

Let the dawn of the year arise!

Scot Bradbury

MEMORIES

Ask what I remember and I know what I see,
Images and thoughts of you and me,
Seen a lot and known a lot, but these things remain
The same, like your name and my pain
When you're not around to be seen.
These memories are eternal like the grass is green.

Seeing is believing and I know what I remember,
Pictures as vivid in my mind as a white December,
Whether snow or sun, or hail or rain,
Being here is nothing but a gain
For my mind. As I visualise the times we've had,
I know that this can't be a futile fad,
Everything I recall; everything is real,
These are my memories that no one can steal.

James Beckett

WHAT IS MAN?

Give me a man who is good, as well as handsome
Who knows his own mind, so will not succumb
To any flattery or the wiles of other women.

Give me a man who knows his own heart
Who also knows what he wants in a woman to be
his other half.
Has moral rectitude and looks to God
in following any path.

Give me a man so capable and so just
Who has wisdom and knowledge and whom God does trust
Is romantic but not pedantic and very, very honest.

Give me a man who woos me and wins me with loving
Without any words but his look so full of knowing
Discovers himself I chose and this, without conversing.

Give me a man whose vows to His God fulfil
Who puts His laws first, his own needs last, until
God gives him freedom and blessing, His will.

God give all women a man like Ian
But not him of course, because to me He is owning
All of the promises as yet unfulfilled for all these years,
now forty-two totalling.

Gerasim

PRISON

Here I sit in my prison,
A prison that has no bars.
A prison with no walls,
Just boundaries.
Oh, how I wish I could be free.
Free to be where I want to be.
The place where I can be me.

Here I stand in my prison,
The prison that engulfs me.
Oh, how I wish the wind would free me.
Free me from my prison.
The wind that knows of no boundaries,
The wind that travels where it pleases.
Please, release me to the wind of my fantasy.

Here I lay in my prison.
The prison that surrounds me.
The prison that is all around me,
The prison that has taken my identity.
Please, let the wind carry me,
So I too can be free!
Free to know me.

Mark Spencer

GOOD PAL, PAT McCALL

(Dedicated to Pat McCall, Engineer,
Midland Hotel 1975 to 1994.
Died of Cancer 2001)

With a prayer gone to Heaven,
Walking through his eternity
Pat gazed upon his mortal self:
The Earth he shall lie within forever,
As dust, as dust, Brandwood End,
With a prayer, gone to Heaven.

Edmund Saint George Mooney

NEED: TO HAVE TO HAVE SOMETHING; TO WANT SOMETHING VERY MUCH

I need you to be my friend
I need you to help me mend

I need you to laugh with me
I need you to look after me

I need you to be there for me
I need you to care for me

I need your arms around me
I need your love to surround me

I need you to be my lover
I need you like no other

I need your time
I need you to be mine

I need you . . . to need me

Gillian L Wise

NEVER TOO LATE

An old lady went shopping
With her purse and a list
Her memory wasn't too good
But she remembered her way to the store in the town
Where she usually purchased her food.

She stood by the door but she couldn't go in
Her purse and her list, they were gone
She couldn't recall where she'd last put them down
And she wished that she'd never left home.

Up came the old gent with the wonderful smile
The one she had met on the bus
He'd picked up her things that she'd left on her seat
And he'd managed to find her at last.

The old lady went shopping
With her purse and a list
Until all of her money was spent
She took home all her shopping in carrier bags
And she also took home the old gent.

Doug Oakley

FANTASY

I appeared to be in a time capsule entering deep space.
Was I dreaming? In any case, it was real to

Me, never before had this taken place. Very hard to explain
this wonderful feeling and elation, I appear

to be on a mission, a voyage beyond the known galaxy.
Was this my vocation, to bring back proof and

specification? Had I been watching too much Star-Trek?
Where no man has ever been before! Or had I just

happened to go through another door? This was the mystery
surrounding the whole episode, travelling through

space. Where was I going in such a terrific haste?
Then I came down to Earth with a bang, I must have

been hallucinating! Was it the drink I'd had the night before?
Someone playing a prank? I will never know.

Anyway it was pleasant while it lasted, that's about all I can say.
I only hope it won't come back another day.

Matthew Wilson

GHOSTLY LAUGHTER

Ghostly laughter, thrills and chills
someone is crying, another is killed

Ghostly laughter, loves to scare
ripping you open, always there

Ghostly laughter never ceases
It shreds you up into little pieces

Ghostly laughter keeps you awake
frightening you until daybreak

Ghostly laughter sails through the air
wrapping its fingers around your hair

Ghostly laughter will never save
making you wish you were in your grave.

Ghostly laughter, someone said
never stops until you're dead!

Sheena Harris

CALL YOURSELF A LEADER?

Call yourself a leader, you're a cheeky bleeder
Check your reputation in the local reader

You're distracted by your own culture
Ignorance, dishonesty and that of a vulture

You have a privileged and honoured position
The people you serve are not your acquisition

Have you forgotten why you are here
Maybe it's time you took a different steer?

Can you remember why you came to power?
Can you tell when it's all going sour?

How do you think you'll be remembered, as someone great?
How you will actually be remembered is open to debate

We need you like people need to be caught unawares
Your behaviour often attracts open mouths and long stares

We need you like people need to be deceived
You carry on as if everything should be believed

We need you like people need no education
Who are you to decide if we deserve an explanation?

We need you like people need to be used
Our intelligence and respect is often abused

We need you like people need no care
Do you understand the meaning of being fair?

We need you like people need to gloat
What message do you think you promote?

We need you like people need a continuous problem
Your actions set an example and others adopt them

We achieve in spite of and not because, of you
You would be wise to take a different view

Your actions profit your own future
The people in your charge salute yer (two fingers)

Ned Dagwilo

HEARTS DON'T LIE

A thousand roses in my heart
are blossoming for you,
a thousand hearts in every rose
will prove my love is true
and all the birds that fly and sing
will testify to this.
I need so much to hold you tight
and live a life of bliss!

I need my love, to see your smile,
to put away your fears.
I need to kiss your lovely eyes
and wipe away your tears,
but most of all to make you feel,
our love grows through the years.

Michael J Pantelides

SHADOW STALKER

Shadows of darkness blind my sight,
They take away my will to fight,
I scream in pain and bow down to fear,
When I feel your presence near.
My tears of blood are streaming down,
I wait in fear and make no sound,
You call me in the dead of night,
Waiting for you to take my life.
The smell of death is lingering near,
The screams of torture are all I can hear,
I'm bound to you, my life is yours,
As I fall onto the dark, cold floor.
Your voice, it pierces through my heart,
I smile, I know that it's the start,
Of a new beginning, a time of peace.
The light is shining on you and me,
The heavens are opening, my soul is yours,
I leave my body bleeding on the floor,
Goodbye to pain, goodbye to fear,
Don't be afraid, I'm always here.

Amanda Hart

RECOGNITION

We take things all for granted
That we should see and write
And hear the sound of laughter
To share a troubled night

Those gifts of loving beauty
We see as flowers grow
And smell the scented perfume
A smell we all should know

The skill of special doctors
The nurse that's always there
To wipe away the teardrops
To brush aside your hair

We can hear the lilted laughter
See the shamrock green
And take it all for granted
And passes by unseen

The loves of loving children
Shared by you and me
Are not just acts of mercy
Or of the things we see

But acts of human kindness
And things you cannot hide
Nothing can be greater
Than he who really tried

E F Croker

APARTHEID

They think they're better
Because of the colour of their skin.
It's the way of life in the country they live in,
People are shot
In the middle of the street.
White people only see one thing
In the faces they meet,
They are blinded by hatred
In everything they do.
They haven't learned how to love their neighbour
Like me and you.

We've only got one world,
One turn
One chance.
So let's get it right
And kill this thing called hate.
Why should it matter
The colour of my mate?
He lives and breathes
Just like me.
So why shouldn't he be
Treated equally?

Éanán Kerr

LOVE FOR GRANTED

Sad and in worries
I find my faith
in my deepest dream
which I cannot stay
banging and hitting on the grave
that bears my name

In my saddest dream
I never saw this thing
that made me mone
in the morning fog

I only see myself in a memory lane
trying not to live the life I once saw

I woke up in the morning sun
and found you like a baby boy
in my past life you were never there
but in this one you felt so real

So I took you in and made you clean
at your first step we were all but friends
I look into your eyes and saw the light
that shone so bright

And in you second step
it was more than a mere smile
in which we giggle and chat

We found our link and binded so quick
strong and firm with style and pride
better than any cast you could find

But for time perfection
was a blink of an eye
I was so blind and taken over
by these new things in my life
I thought everything was so right
then it happened . . .
I was struck by lightning
in the stroke of morning

And a thousand pieces of my heart
floating with the dust
and at the sleeping sun

I was all alone on my bed in black
with a word that twisted my mind
called faith

Although I knew for now
my work was taken for granted
I have foreseen and await the day
you are going to stand before me
like a scarecrow.

Omolei Asikhia